Microsoft®

Word
2010

made
easy

Which? Books are commissioned and published by Which? Ltd,
2 Marylebone Road, London NW1 4DF
Email: books@which.co.uk

British Library Cataloguing in Publication Data
A catalogue record for this book is available from the British Library

ISBN 978 1 84490 144 9

1 3 5 7 9 10 8 6 4 2

Consultant editor: Lynn Wright
Project manager: Emma Callery
Designer: Blanche Williams, Harper Williams Ltd
Proofreader: Sian Stark
Indexer: Christine Bernstein
Printed and bound by Charterhouse, Hatfield
Distributed by Littlehampton Book Services Ltd, Faraday Close, Durrington, Worthing, West Sussex
BN13 3RB

Essential Velvet is an elemental chlorine-free paper produced at Condat in Périgord, France using
timber from sustainably managed forests. The mill is ISO14001 and EMAS certified.

For a full list of Which? Books, please call 01903 828557 or access our website at www.which.co.uk,
or write to Littlehampton Book Services.

Which?

Microsoft®

Word 2010

made easy

4

Contents

Get Started

Page navigation and layout

Work with text

Photos and graphics

Do more with Word

Resources

Editorial note

The instructions in this guide refer to the Windows 7 operating system and Microsoft Office Home and Student 2010.

Screenshots are used for illustrative purposes only.

Windows 7 and Microsoft Office Home and Student 2010 are American products. All spellings on the screenshots and on the buttons and boxes in the text are therefore spelled in US English. The rest of the text remains in UK English.

All technical words in the book are either discussed in jargon busters within the text and/or can be found in the Jargon Buster section on pages 153-5.

When asked to click on something, note that this means a left click unless specified otherwise.

Introduction

Microsoft Word is one of the world's most popular writing software programs. Used in schools, businesses and at home, it is a rich word-processing tool that is suitable for writing everything from a homework essay, letter to a bank, or even a family newsletter. Hidden beneath the standard word-processing tools are deep features that will help you save time, add polish to your documents, and give you more control over your word processing needs.

Word 2010 Made Easy takes you on a step-by-step journey that helps you get more from your word processing. Beginning with first steps that get you started with Word and become familiar with its interface and controls, this book then ventures into learning more powerful layout and text-editing tools, to formatting your text and using templates.

When you're ready for more adventurous tutorials, *Word 2010 Made Easy* can help you add zing to your documents with photos and graphics. Learn how to add and edit images, work with shapes and special effects, understand the power of SmartArt graphics, and even add tables for professional layouts. And there's no point keeping the good work you've learnt to yourself. *Word 2010 Made Easy* also helps you share your documents, track and review changes, and protect documents to stop them being edited.

Word 2010 Made Easy will help you get the best from Microsoft Word, and also includes a handy guide to Word's keyboard shortcuts as well as a comprehensive jargon buster that explains any technical terms in plain English. Now that you're ready to make the most of Word, let's get started.

Get started

By reading this chapter you'll get to grips with:

- Opening new and existing documents
- Working with the Ribbon
- Saving documents in different formats

Office Suites

For many people, the ability to create professional looking office documents is one of the main reasons they bought a computer. Whether it's using a word processor to write a letter or a spreadsheet to calculate household finances, these tasks are made easier by using suitable software.

While your computer may have come with a very basic word processor, such as Wordpad (which comes built into Windows), investing in an office software suite is something that most users should consider if they are going to make the most of their computer.

An office suite is a bundle of computer programs for doing common tasks such as writing letters and managing budgets. Originally, office suites were designed with professional office workers in mind. However, with the growing trend towards working from home and the increasing use of the computer at home in general, software manufacturers now create versions of office suites with the home user in mind.

Tip

OpenOffice at www.openoffice.org is a good alternative choice for anyone wanting a full-featured office suite free of charge. It's what's known as open source software, so you can download and install the software at no cost. The website encourages you to contribute to the ongoing development of the software, donating time or money to help it progress.

The best-known office suite on the market is Microsoft Office, which is available in several versions to suit different needs and budgets. It contains familiar Microsoft programs such as Word (word processor), Excel (a spreadsheet program) and PowerPoint (a presentations package).

Get started with Word

Before creating your first document, it's worth spending a little time getting to know Word's workspace. The key tools and commands you need can be found on the Backstage view, the Quick Access Toolbar or on the Ribbon.

Backstage view

Here you'll find various options for opening, saving, printing or sharing a document. To get to the Backstage view:

1 Click the **Start** button.

2 Click **All Programs** and then click **Microsoft Word**. A new blank document will open automatically.

3 Click the **File** tab.

4 Choose an option on the left side of the page, such as **Info**.

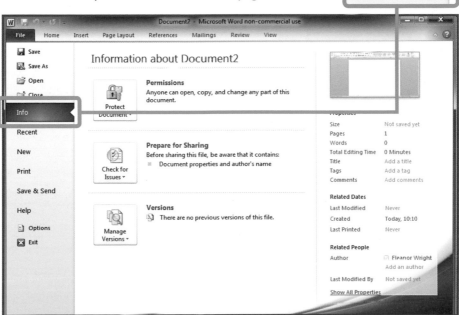

5 To return to your document, click any tab on the Ribbon (see pages 11–12).

Get started

Quick Access Toolbar

This sits above the Ribbon (see overleaf), and offers fast access to common commands such as 'Save', 'Undo' and 'Repeat'. You can also add other commands to make working in Word easier.

1 Click the **drop-down arrow** that lies to the right of the Quick Access Toolbar.

2 Select the command you want to add from the drop-down menu and it will appear in the Quick Access Toolbar.

3 If the command you want to add isn't there, click **More Commands...** to see more listed.

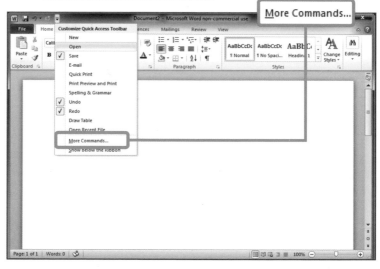

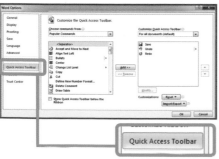

4 In the dialog box that opens, the list box on the right shows the commands that are currently on the Quick Access Toolbar. The list box on the left shows the commands you can add. In the 'Choose Commands from:' field click the **down arrow** and select **All Commands** to see a full list of the commands available.

5 Select a command and click the **Add** button that sits between the two boxes. The command will then be added to the Quick Access Toolbar.

The Ribbon

The Ribbon that appears at the top of your Word window features all the commands you need to make changes to your document. It contains multiple tabs, each with several and related groups of commands. You can also add your own tabs containing your favourite commands (see pages 13-15). Some groups have an arrow in the bottom-right corner. When you click the arrow, you can get access to even more commands.

The Home tab

This houses the basic formatting tools. From here, you can change the style, size and colour of your text, create bulleted and numbered lists and more. Find out how to use these on pages 50-60.

The Insert tab

Insert other elements into your document such as pictures and shapes (see pages 90-5 and 106). You can also add headers and footers or the date and time (see pages 36-7).

The Page Layout tab

Change the orientation of your page from vertical (portrait - usually the default setting) to horizontal (landscape), create multiple columns of text or add borders to your page.

The References tab

A great tab full of tools that are useful for anyone writing long research documents or papers. These include inserting endnotes and footnotes into long documents or creating a table of contents.

The Mailings tab

Create labels and envelopes, or do a mail merge (see pages 142–4).

The Review tab

Check the contents of your document using the spellchecker or access the thesaurus. You can also 'Track Changes', which lets you see the changes that you or others have made to a document (see pages 145–8).

The View tab

Zoom in or out on documents to make them easier to view. You can also see how your document will look when printed or published online as well as when displayed in draft mode - plain text with no formatting.

Tip

Along with the seven main tabs, further contextual tool tabs appear on the Ribbon, depending on your actions in Word. For example, if you click in a table, two extra Table Tools tabs appear – one for Design and one for Layout. These contain the controls you need to format items. Similar contextual tab tools appear if you click on a picture, edit a header or footer, or click in a text box.

Customise the Ribbon

You can change the Ribbon to suit the way you work in Word. For example, you can create new tabs with the commands you use most often on them. Commands are housed within a group, and you can create as many groups as you need to keep your tab organised. You can also add commands to any of the default tabs, provided you first create a custom group in the tab.

1 Right click the Ribbon and select **Customize the Ribbon...**.

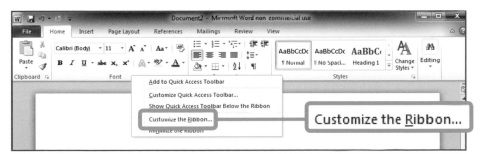

2 In the dialog box that appears, click **New Tab**. A new tab will be created with a new group inside it.

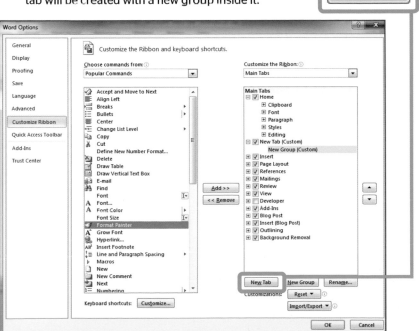

3 Click on the new tab in the dialog box and then **Rename...** so you can give it a more descriptive name.

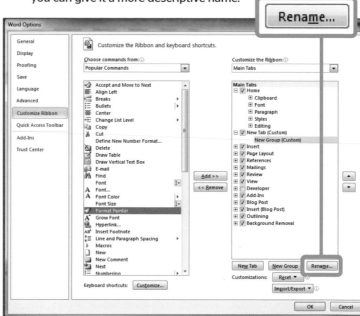

4 Under the new renamed tab, click **New Group (Custom)**.

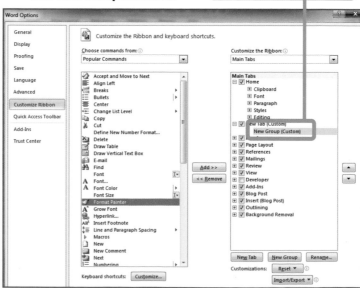

5 Select a command from the list on the left, then click **Add**. You can also drag commands directly into a group.

6 If you can't see the command you want, click on the arrow below 'Choose commands from', and click **All Commands**.

7 Use the arrow keys to order your commands exactly the way you want them to appear on the Ribbon tab. In this case, up means left and down means right.

8 When you have finished adding commands, click **OK**.

Shrink the Ribbon

If you find that the Ribbon is taking up too much screen space you can choose to minimise it.

1 Click the arrow in the upper-right corner of the Ribbon to minimise it.

2 To maximise the Ribbon, click the arrow again.

When the Ribbon is minimised, you can make it reappear by clicking on a tab. However, the Ribbon will disappear again when you're not using it.

Use the Status bar

At the bottom of the Word window is the Status bar, which provides useful information about your document including word count, page number, line number, zoom, zoom slider and the language used.

Word makes it easy to customise the Status bar so it shows only the information you want.

Customise the Status bar

1 Right click anywhere on the Status bar.

2 A pop-up menu appears listing all the options available. You'll see ticks in the left column that indicate the options already active.

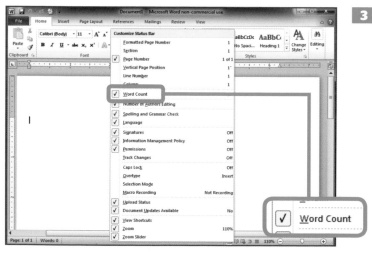

3 To turn on an option, such as word count, simply click in the left column next to its name and a tick will appear. To disable an option, click on the tick mark in the left column to make it disappear.

4 Upon clicking, you'll see the respective info either appear in the Status bar or disappear from the Status bar.

Create and open a document

To create a new, blank document in Word:

1 Open Microsoft Word – there may be an icon on the desktop or taskbar. If not, search for it by clicking on **Start**.

2 A new blank document will open automatically. If you already have a document open and want to create a new document, click **File**.

3 This shows the Backstage view (see page 9). Here are the commands you use to manage and apply changes to your document. Click **New**.

4 The Blank document option under 'Available Templates' will be highlighted by default. Click **Create**.

5 A blank document, which looks like a white sheet of paper, will appear taking up most of the window. Above this document sits the Ribbon.

6 You can start typing.

Open an existing document

1 Click **File** to go to the Backstage view.

2 Click **Open**. The 'Open' dialog box will appear showing folders and files on your computer hard drive.

3 Select a document and then click **Open**.

4 If you've opened a file recently, you can access it from the **Recent Documents** list. Click on the **File** tab and select **Recent**.

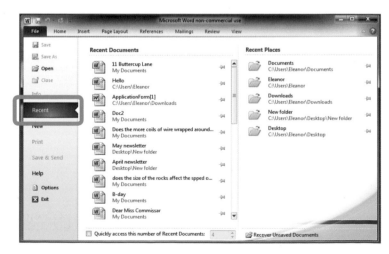

Open previous version documents

When you open a document created in an earlier version of Word (Word 2007 or Word 97-2003) it will open in compatibility mode. This is indicated by the words '[Compatibility Mode]' that follow the document name in the title bar.

Working in compatibility mode disables Word 2010's new features and preserves the original layout of the document so that it can be still edited by users of previous versions of Word. If the title bar does not display '[Compatibility Mode]', the document is in Word 2010 mode and all features are available.

You can choose to work and save a document in compatibility mode or convert it to Word 2010's .docx format. By converting the document, you gain full access to Word 2010's new features and the document layout will appear as if it had been created in this version of Word.

Convert a document to Word 2010 mode

1 With the document open, click the **File** tab.

2 If you want to convert the document without saving a copy, click **Info**, and then click **Convert**.

Get started

3 A dialog box will appear alerting you to possible changes in your document layout if you proceed. Click **OK**.

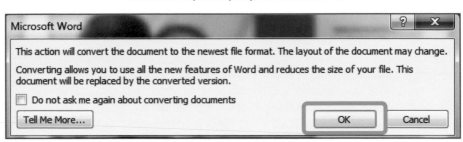

4 To create a new copy of the document in Word 2010 mode, click **Save As**, give the document a name in the 'File name' box (see also opposite), and select **Word Document** in the 'Save as type' list.

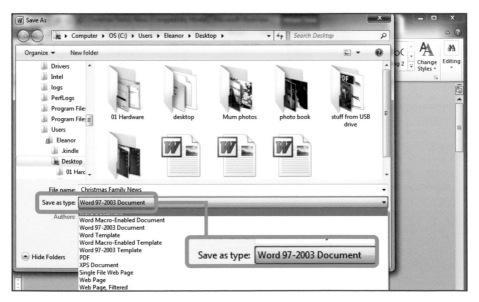

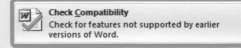

Tip

If the words '[Compatibility Mode]' appear in the title bar of a document window, the document is either a Word 2007 or Word 97-2003 file. To check which version, click the **File** tab and then **Info**. In the 'Prepare for Sharing' section, click **Check for Issues**, and then click **Check Compatibility**. Now click **Select versions to show**.

Save a document

1 Click **File**, then click **Save**. If this is the first time you've saved your document, the 'Save As' dialog box will open.

2 'Save As' lets you choose a name and location for your document. The default location for saving files is the Documents folder. By default too, Word will suggest a file name for your document based on the first few words in your document.

3 Click **Save** if you're happy with these default settings.

4 If, at step 2, you wish to save your document to a different location, use the shortcuts on the left-hand side of the 'Save As' dialog box to select a new location.

5 If, at step 2, you want to name your document yourself, click in the **File name** box to highlight the default name and type the name of your choice.

6 Click **Save**. If you've saved your document previously but want to give it a new name, select **Save As** from the 'File' tab drop-down menu, rename it and then click **Save**.

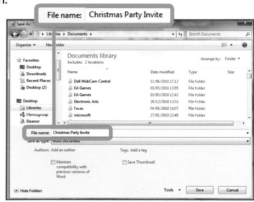

Save as an older format

You can share your documents with anyone using Word 2010 or 2007, as they use the same .docx file format. However, older versions of Word use a different file format. To ensure your documents can be opened and read using a previous version of Microsoft Word, you need to save it as a Word 97-2003 Document. Here's how:

1 Click **File**, then click **Save As**.

2 In the 'Save As' dialog, click the 'Save as type' **drop-down arrow**.

3 From the drop-down menu, select **Word 97-2003 Document**. Click **Save**.

Open or save in another format

You can use Word 2010 to open or save files in a range of other formats. For example, you can open an OpenDocument Text (an open source file format used by some word processors) or a WordPerfect file (a word processing program) or even a web page, and then use Word 2010 to make edits.

Open a non-Word file

1 Click the **File** tab.

2 Click **Open**.

3 In the 'Open' dialog box, click the down arrow next to 'All Word Documents' and select the type of file that you want to open.

> Works 6 - 9 Document
>
> All Word Documents ▼

All Files
All Word Documents
Word Documents
Word Macro-Enabled Documents
XML Files
Word 97-2003 Documents
All Web Pages
All Word Templates
Word Templates
Word Macro-Enabled Templates
Word 97-2003 Templates
Rich Text Format
Text Files
OpenDocument Text
Recover Text from Any File
WordPerfect 5.x
WordPerfect 6.x
Works 6 - 9 Document
All Word Documents

4 Select the file and then click **Open** at the foot of the dialog box.

Save a Word document in another file format

1 Click the **File** tab.

2 Click **Save As**.

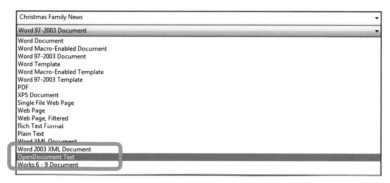

3 In the 'Save As' dialog box, click the 'Save as type' **drop-down arrow** and then click the file type that you want.

File type	File format
Word Document	.docx
Word Macro-Enabled Document	**.docm**
Word 97-2003 Document	.doc
Word Template	**.dotx**
Word Macro-Enabled Template	.dotm
Word 97-2003 Template	**.dot**
PDF	.pdf
XPS Document	**.XPS**
Single File Web Page	.mht (MHTML)
Web Page	**.htm**
Web Pag, Filtered	.htm (HTML filtered)
Rich Text Format	**.rtf**
Plain Text	.txt
Word XML Document	**.xml (Word 2007)**
Word 2003 XML Document	.xml (Word 2003)
OpenDocument Text	**.odt**
Works 6 - 9 Document	.wps

4 Type a name for the document in the **File name** box (see page 21).

5 Click **Save** (see page 21).

> **Jargon buster**
> **File format** Refers to the specific way that information is stored within a computer file. The letters that appear after the file name show what type of file it is and what type of program will open it – for example, a Microsoft Word file will end in .docx, while a Microsoft Excel file will end in .xlsx.

Save a document as a PDF

If you need to share a Word document with other people who do not have Word (or may have different versions or fonts), or the document has lots of images and is therefore very large in terms of file size, you can save it in the .pdf file format.

Portable Document Format or PDF is a file format that can be opened on any type of computer or device using Adobe's free Adobe Reader software – no matter what software or type of computer was originally used to create the file. As it compresses data, a PDF file is much smaller than the original document making it easier to share via email or upload online.

Furthermore, a PDF file accurately shows the original document layout complete with fonts, colours and images.

You may have seen PDF documents already, as it's the most popular file format for sharing digital information. It is commonly used for online documents, manuals, government publications, leaflets, forms and downloadable menus from websites – and many ebooks and digital magazines are available as PDFs.

Word 2010 has a built-in PDF writer so you can create a PDF with a few clicks. There are two ways to do this in Word 2010. You can use the 'Save As' function and select the .pdf format or use the 'Share' menu and choose the option to create a PDF document.

Create a PDF

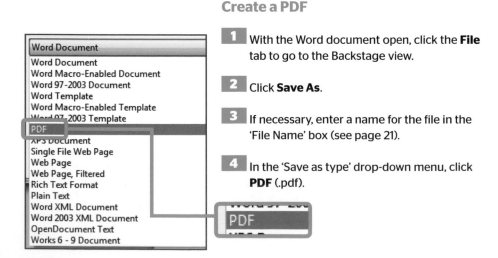

1 With the Word document open, click the **File** tab to go to the Backstage view.

2 Click **Save As**.

3 If necessary, enter a name for the file in the 'File Name' box (see page 21).

4 In the 'Save as type' drop-down menu, click **PDF** (.pdf).

5 When you choose the PDF file type, the following options become available:

- **Optimize for:** affects the file size and quality of the PDF that's created. If you want the smallest file size possible, perhaps for emailing the PDF to someone to read onscreen, choose **Minimum size (publishing online)**. If, at some point, you want a high-quality print of the PDF choose **Standard (publishing online and printing)**.

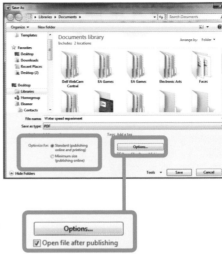

- **Open file after publishing:** tick this box if you want to view the document as a PDF after saving.

6 Click the **Options...** button.

7 In the 'Options' window under 'Page range', you can determine the pages of the document to include in the PDF.

8 Under 'Publish what' you can also choose whether markup (comments) should be printed, and you can select output options in 'Include non-printing information'. Finally, under PDF options, you can choose to bitmap text when you don't have the rights to embed one or more of the fonts in your document. This creates a PDF that looks exactly as you designed it, even if others who view it do not have the same fonts as those used in the original document.

9 Click **OK** when finished, then click **Save**.

BE CAREFUL!

A smaller sized PDF will have poorer quality images, as they will have been highly compressed to create a small file. This won't matter if you intend to view the PDF on screen, but if you intend to print the PDF you won't be able to get a high-quality print. If you're unsure about which 'Optimise for' setting to choose, create a PDF in each option, then compare the two for their image quality and file size.

Recover an unsaved document

It's important to regularly save your document by clicking **File** and then **Save**. Or you can press the keys **Ctrl** and **S** at the same time (indicated by pressing **Ctrl + S**) on your keyboard to perform a save.

Word can automatically save your document at regular intervals using the AutoRecover feature, so should something unexpected happen - such as power outage - or you accidently close a document without saving, a version of your file will be saved.

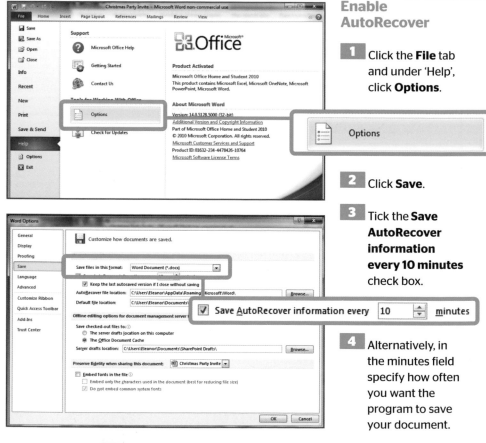

Enable AutoRecover

1 Click the **File** tab and under 'Help', click **Options**.

2 Click **Save**.

3 Tick the **Save AutoRecover information every 10 minutes** check box.

4 Alternatively, in the minutes field specify how often you want the program to save your document.

5 Select the **Keep the last autosaved version if I close without saving** check box.

6 Click **OK**.

Open an autosaved version of your document

1 Open the document that was previously closed without saving.

2 Click **File**.

3 In Backstage view, click **Info**.

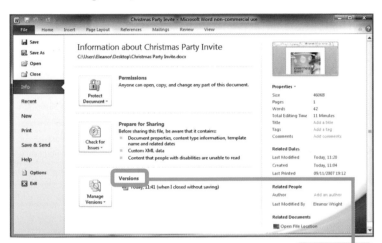

Versions

4 Autosaved versions of your file will appear under 'Versions'. Click on the file to open it.

5 To keep this version, click **Restore**.

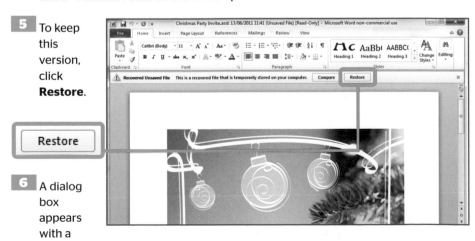

Restore

6 A dialog box appears with a warning that you are about to overwrite the last saved version of that file with the selected version. Click **OK**.

Print a document

Open your document (see page 18), then follow these steps to print out your work with the default settings:

1 Click **File**.

2 Click **Print**. You'll see a preview of what you are about to print on the right-hand side.

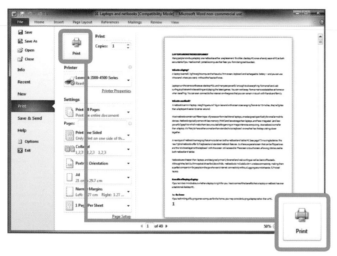

3 Under 'Settings', click on the individual settings to change them from the default. For example, if you wish to print only certain pages of your document, type the range. Otherwise, select **Print All Pages**.

4 Click the **Print** button.

To pick a different printer or printer style

1 To select a different printer, click the down arrow next to the current printer, and click on the one you want to use instead.

2 To make changes to your printer's settings, click **Printer Properties**. Click **Advanced** for more options.

3 Depending on your printer model, you may be able to select which printer tray the paper should come from, change the size of the paper you print on or opt for double-sided printing.

4 Click **OK** when you're happy with the changes you've made.

When you've saved your work, close your document by clicking **File** and then **Close**.

Page navigation and layout

By reading this chapter you'll get to grips with:

- Using and creating templates
- Setting up page layouts
- Working with document views

Use a template

A template is a pre-designed and pre-formatted document that creates a copy of itself when it's opened. Using a template lets you quickly create a document without worrying about page layout and text formatting. Word comes with a range of sample templates that can help save time and effort. Whether you want to create a letter, a flyer, newsletter or form, you can usually find a template to suit.

Open a template

1 Open Word and click the **File** tab to go to the Backstage view.

2 Select **New** to open the 'New Document' pane.

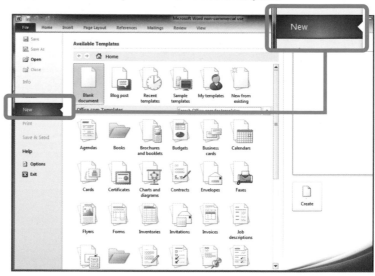

3 Click **Sample templates** to choose a built-in template, or select an 'Office.com Template' category, shown here, to select and download a template from Microsoft's website.

4 Select a template and click **Create**. A new document will appear using the template you've chosen.

Office.com Templates

Insert text into a template

Most templates use placeholder text – sometimes shown surrounded by square brackets – which you replace with your own text.

1 Click on the text you want to replace. The text will appear highlighted.

2 Enter your text. It will replace the placeholder text.

Jargon buster

Placeholder text Also known as dummy text. A piece of text – sometimes nonsense text such as 'lorem ipsum' – designed to show the position, font, size and format of text in a layout.

Create your own template

You can create your own custom template by either making changes to an existing template (see pages 30-1) or by using a Word 2010 document you've already created and formatted.

1 Click the **File** tab and then **Open**. Select the document that you want to use as a template.

2 Check, and adjust if necessary, the page layout's settings such as margins, page size and orientation, styles and text formatting to suit your template (see pages 33-5).

3 Remove any text that doesn't need to be in the template. Leave only the text that you want to appear in all documents based on that template.

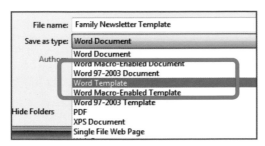

4 Click the **File** tab and then select **Save As**.

5 In the 'Save As' dialog box, click the 'Save as type' **drop-down arrow** and then from the drop-down menu select **Word Template** (.dotx).

6 Type a name into the 'File name' text box. Click **Save**. The template will be saved to the location where Word stores its document templates (see page 30). Click the **File** tab and then click **Close** to close the template.

7 When you want to use this template to create a new document, click the **File** tab and select it from the **New** window.

Tip

There is a quick way to create a new document using an existing Word document as a template. Click the **File** tab and click **New**. Select **New from existing** in the main panel and then choose a Word document to use as a template. Click **Open**. A new, untitled document will open, but all the styles and text from the document you selected as a template will appear in this new document. The original Word document remains untouched.

When giving your template a filename, include 'Template'. For example, naming it 'Family Newsletter Template' instantly shows what type of file it is.

Change the page layout

When you create a new document, the blank page that appears uses Word's default page layout settings. These may not work for the document you wish to create. For example, you may need to change your document's page size to match the size of paper when printing or you may wish to change the page orientation or margins.

Change the page size

1 Click the **Page Layout** tab.

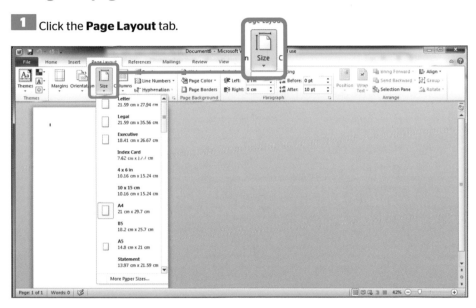

2 In the 'Page Setup' group, click **Size**. A drop-down menu appears with the current page size highlighted.

3 Click the page size you want and the document will change accordingly.

Change page orientation for the entire document

1 Click the **Page Layout** tab.

2 In the 'Page Setup' group, click **Orientation**.

3 Click either **Portrait** or **Landscape** to change the page orientation.

Tip

You can use both portrait or landscape pages in the same Word document. Select the text that needs changing. On the **Page Layout** tab, in the 'Page Setup' group, click **Margins**. Then click **Custom Margins**. On the **Margins** tab, click **Portrait** or **Landscape**. Then in the 'Apply to' drop-down menu, click **Selected text**.

Change the page margins

Page margins are the blank areas around the edges of a page. In most page layouts, text and graphics appear inside these page margins. By changing a document's page margins, you can change where text and graphics appear on each page. You can do this either by selecting one of Word's default settings or by creating your own custom margins.

Change page margins settings

1 Click the **Page Layout** tab.

2 In the 'Page Setup' group, click **Margins**. The Margins gallery appears – with 'Normal' selected by default.

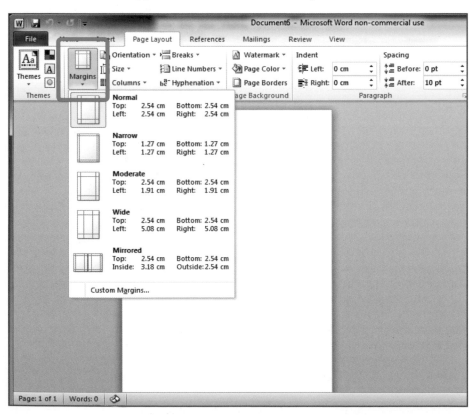

3 Click the margin size you want.

Create custom page margins

1 Click the **Page Layout** tab.

2 In the 'Page Setup' group, click **Margins**.

3 At the bottom of the 'Margins' gallery, click **Custom Margins**.

4 In the 'Page Setup' dialog box that appears, enter new values for the margins. Then click **OK**.

Tip

To change the margins for part of a document, select the text, and then set the margins by entering the new values in the 'Page Setup' dialog box. In 'Apply to box', click **Selected text**.

BE CAREFUL!

Most printers require a minimum margin width, because they can't print to the edge of the page. If your margins are too narrow, you may see the following message 'One or more margins are set outside the printable area of the page.' To avoid text from being cut off, click **Fix to automatically increase the margin width**. Check the manual to find out the minimum settings for your printer.

View page margins

When designing a page layout, it's useful to see the text area. Word can display lines in your document that represent the page margins.

1 On the **File** tab, click **Options**.

2 Click **Advanced**, and then under 'Show document content' select the **Show text boundaries** check box.

3 The page margins will appear in your document as dotted lines.

Use headers and footers

Using headers and footers can make your Word document look more professional. A header is an area that appears at the top of every page, while a footer appears in the bottom margin of every page. They are generally used to show information such as page number, the document name and date.

Add a header or footer

1 Click the **Insert** tab.

2 In the 'Header & Footer' group, click either **Header** or **Footer**.

3 From the drop-down menu, select **Blank** to insert a blank header or footer, or choose one of the other preformatted options.

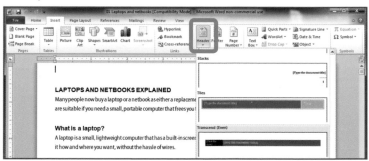

4 The 'Design' tab will appear on the Ribbon, and the header or footer will appear in the document.

Tip
To edit a footer or header, click the **Insert** tab and, in the 'Header & Footer' group, choose **Header>Edit Header**.

5 Type in the text you wish to appear into the header or footer. If placeholder text exists, click on it and type the replacement text.

6 Click **Close Header and Footer** in the 'Design' tab.

Add the date or time into a header or footer

1 Double click anywhere on the header or footer to unlock it. The 'Design' tab will appear.

2 From the **Design** tab and in the 'Insert' group, click

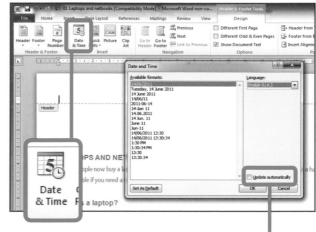

Date & Time. Select a date and/or time format in the dialog box.

3 Tick the **Update automatically** box if you want it to reflect the current date and time. Otherwise it will not update to show the correct information when the document is opened at a later stage.

☐ Update automatically

4 Click **OK**. The date/time now appears in the document.

Add page numbers

When creating a large document with several pages, you may want to add page numbers to keep them in order. You can use headers and footers to automatically add page numbers to your document when printed.

1 Click the **Insert** tab and, in the 'Header & Footer' area, click **Page Number**.

2 A drop-down menu appears. From here you can choose where you want the page numbers to appear in the document and what format they will take. Click on a location for your page numbers such as **Top of Page**, **Bottom of Page** and **Page Margins** (side of the page).

3 Next, choose a page-numbering style. There are lots of numbering styles to choose from so scroll fully through the list before you choose. Click on the **Design** tab and then **Close Header and Footer** (under 'Header & Footer Tools').

Add a page background

You can jazz up your Word document by adding a background to the pages. You can choose a colour or image, or even use special effects such as gradients, patterns or textures.

1 Open the Word document that you wish to add a background to.

2 Click the **Page Layout** tab, and in the 'Page Background' group, click **Page Color**.

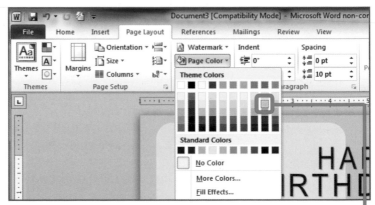

3 Move your cursor over a colour to see a live preview.

4 Click **More Colors...** to see additional colours, Click a colour to apply it.

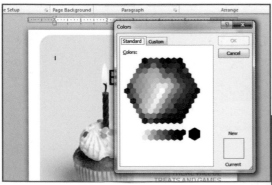

5 Click **Fill Effects...** in the 'Page Color' drop-down menu to apply a gradient, pattern, or texture or choose a picture to use as a background image.

Apply a picture as a background

1 With the Word document open, click the **Page Layout** tab, and in the 'Page Background' group, click **Page Color**.

2 Click **Fill Effects...**.

3 In the 'Fill Effects' dialog box, click the **Picture** tab and then click **Select Picture...**.

4 In the 'Select Picture' dialog window, select the picture you wish to use and click **Insert**.

5 The image will appear in the dialog box, now click **OK**.

6 The image will be used in the background.

Add a page border

Give your Word document a distinctive look by adding page borders. You can choose the style, colour and width of a border to customise your own look or use a pre-designed border.

1 Open the Word document to which you wish to add a background.

2 Place your cursor on the page to which you want to add a border.

3 Click the **Page Layout** tab and, in the 'Page Background' group, click **Page Borders**.

4 In the 'Borders and Shading' dialog box, select the **Page Border** tab – if it's not already selected.

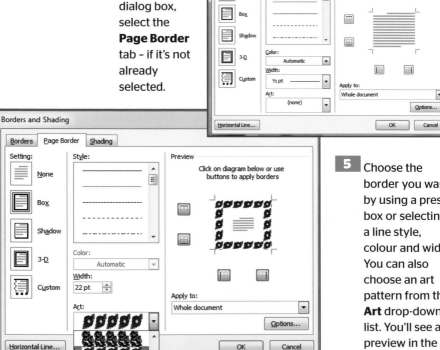

5 Choose the border you want by using a preset box or selecting a line style, colour and width. You can also choose an art pattern from the **Art** drop-down list. You'll see a preview in the right-hand pane of the dialog box.

6 You can click on the four buttons in this right-hand 'Preview' pane: Top, Bottom, Left and Right to add/remove the border on those sides.

7 Now choose the pages of your Word document that you wish to add the border to by clicking the **Apply To** drop-down list. You can, for example, put a border on every page by selecting **Whole Document** or choosing **This Section– First Page Only** to add a border to the first page.

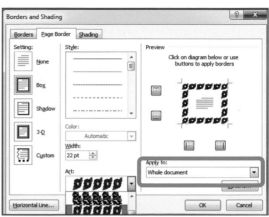

8 Click the **Options...** button on the 'Page Border' dialog box to open the 'Border and Shading Options' dialog box. Here you can select the margins of the border, either from the text or from the page edges, and preview the border layout.

9 Click **OK** to close the 'Options' dialog box.

10 Click **OK** to close the 'Borders and Shading' dialog box.

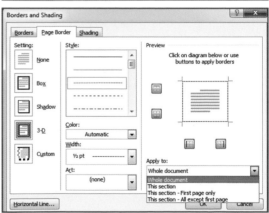

Tip
You may find that when printing your document, the page borders print incorrectly. If this happens, choose the **Text** option in the 'Measure From' drop-down list in the 'Border and Shading Options' dialog box (Step 8). Increase the values in the Margin area to give a border based on the edges of the page. It should now print correctly.

Change document views

You can change the way you view your document by clicking the relevant icon in the 'Document View' group on the **View** tab.

Print Layout

This is the default view that Word uses to display your document. It shows what your document will look like when printed. This view is suitable for when you need to adjust

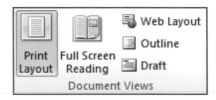

margins and columns, headers and footers, as well as for work with images, text boxes and frames. Useful for: general editing.

Full Screen Reading

Designed to make on-screen reading more comfortable, this view shows your document in large pages across the whole screen without the normal menus. You can use the tools at the top of the screen to add comments or highlight text. This view does not show how the document will be printed: text may look larger than expected, and page breaks may not match printed pages breaks. Useful for: reading large documents.

Web Layout

Shows how your document will look as a web page with visible backgrounds, text that wraps to the window and graphics positioned as if in a Web browser. Useful for: creating web pages.

Outline

This view lets you look at the structure of your document. You can collapse a document to see only the main headings or expand it to see all headings and even body text. You can then move, copy, and reorganise text by dragging headings up or down the document. However, you must first assign heading and paragraph styles to your text for this feature to work (see pages 83–6). Useful for: Working with long documents with multiple chapters or creating a master document.

Draft

The default in earlier versions of Word, this view shows your text without full page formatting such as headers and footers. Placeholders for any pictures, tables, text boxes and frames may be shown. Useful for: quick editing of text.

Work with text

By reading this chapter you'll get to grips with:

- ◼ Formatting text
- ◼ Working with columns
- ◼ Using styles and themes

Add text to a document

Learn the basics of working with text in Word – from inserting and deleting text to cutting and pasting selected text.

Add text

The cursor, a blinking vertical line in the upper-left corner of the page, shows you where the words you type will appear on the page.

1 If you want to start typing further down the page, press the **Enter** key on your keyboard until the cursor is where you want to type.

2 Alternatively, move your mouse to the location you wish text to appear in the document and click the mouse. The cursor will appear here.

3 Start typing.

Select text

1 Move your cursor next to the text you wish to select.

2 Click and hold down the mouse button while dragging the cursor over the text to select it.

3 Release the mouse button. A highlighted box will appear over the selected text.

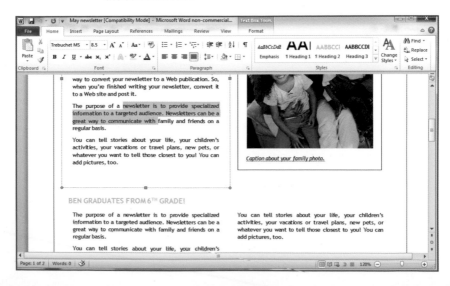

Delete text

1 Move your cursor next to the text you wish to delete.

2 Press the **Backspace** key on your keyboard to delete text to the left of the cursor.

3 Press the **Delete** key on your keyboard to delete text to the right of the cursor.

Copy and paste text

1 Select the text you wish to copy.

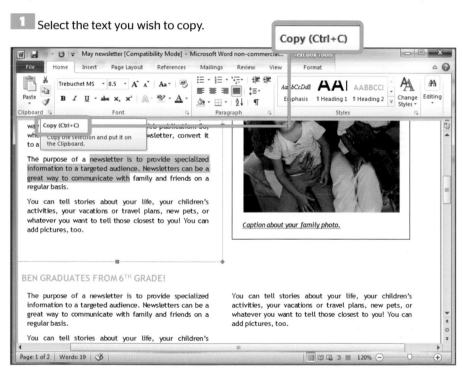

2 Click the **Home** tab, then **Copy**.

3 Place your cursor where you wish the text to appear.

4 Click the **Home** tab, then **Paste**. The text will appear.

Cut and paste text

1 Select the text you wish to cut.

2 Click the **Home** tab, then **Cut**. The text will be 'cut' from the document, and disappear.

Cut (Ctrl+X)

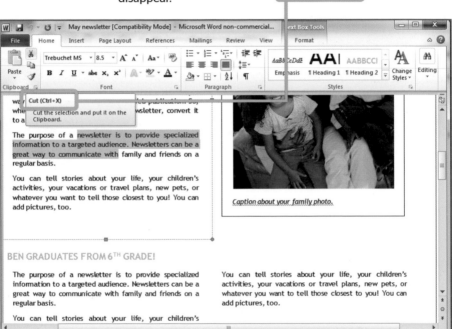

3 Place your cursor where you wish the text to reappear.

4 Click the **Home** tab, then **Paste** for the text to appear.

Tip

When you select text or images in Word, a hover toolbar appears. This contains the main formatting commands. If it doesn't show at first, move your mouse over the selection.

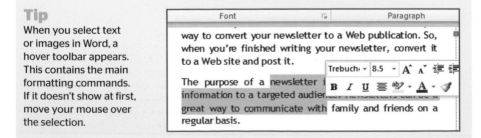

Format text

To create good-looking documents that capture your readers' attention, you can change the way your text looks from Word's default settings. Word's formatting tools let you customise everything from the style of font, size and colour of text right through to its alignment and placement.

Change the size of text

1 Select the text you wish to change. On the **Home** tab, in the 'Font' group, click the 'Font Size' **drop-down arrow**.

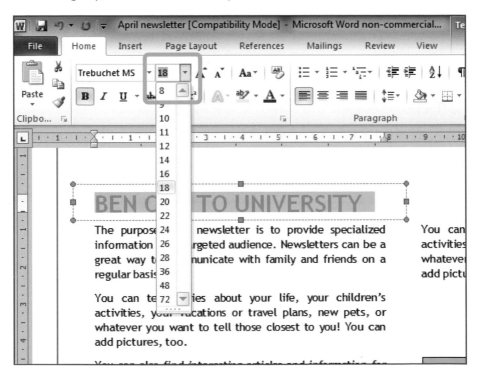

2 From the drop-down menu select a font size. When you move your cursor over each font size, a live preview of the sized text will appear in the document.

Tip

To remove text formatting, select the text that you want to clear the formats from (or press **Ctrl + A** to select everything in the document), then on the **Home** tab, in the 'Font' group, click **Clear Formatting**.

Change the font

1 Select the text you wish to change.

2 On the **Home** tab, in the 'Font' group, click the **drop-down arrow** next to the 'Font' box.

3 From the 'Font' drop-down menu, select a font. As you move the cursor over a font in the list, the selected text in the document will change so you can preview each font.

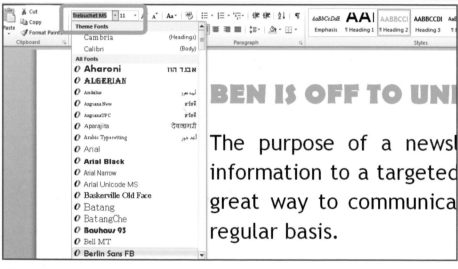

Change the colour of text

1 Select the text you want to change.

2 On the **Home** tab, in the 'Font' group, click the 'Font Color' **drop-down arrow**.

3 From the 'Font Color' menu, select a new colour. As you move your cursor over a colour the selected text in the document will change so you can preview each colour.

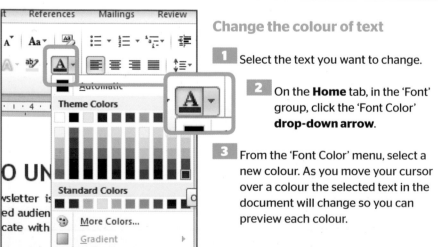

Use the Bold, Italic and Underline commands

1 Select the text you wish to change.

2 On the **Home** tab, in the 'Font' group, click the **Bold** (B), **Italic** (I), or **Underline** (U) command.

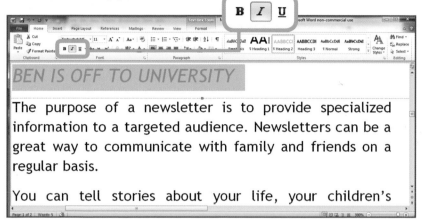

Change the text case

1 Select the text you want to change.

2 On the **Home** tab, in the 'Font' group, click **Change Case**.

3 Select an option, such as **UPPERCASE**, from the list.

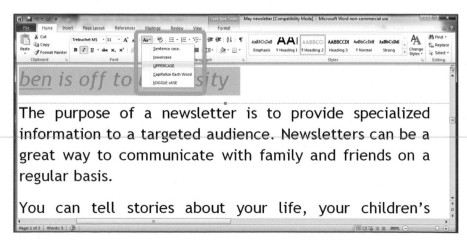

Format paragraphs

With the paragraph section of the Home tab you can alter the layout of your text in paragraphs.

Change text alignment

By default, Word aligns text to the left-hand side of the page, but you can change this to align text to the right page margin, centre your text or justify text so that a paragraph lines up equally to the right and left margins.

> If you don't see the horiontal ruler, click **Ruler** on the **View** tab.

1 Select the text you wish to modify.

2 Click the **Home** tab.

3 Select one of the four following alignment options from the 'Paragraph' group:

- **Align Text Left:** Aligns all selected text to the left margin.
- **Center:** Aligns text an equal distance from the left and right margins.
- **Align Text Right:** Aligns all selected text to the right margin.
- **Justify:** Justified text is equal on both sides and lines up against the right and left margins.

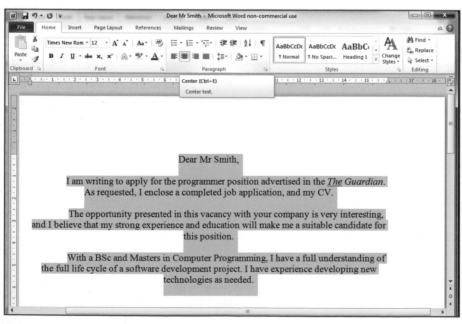

Work with tabs

Tabs are a great way to accurately position text in your document. Every time you press the tab key on your keyboard, your cursor moves half an inch to the right by default. By adding different tab stops to the ruler you can change the position and alignment of tabs. The types of tab stops available include:

- **Left Tab:** left-aligns the text at the tab stop.
- **Center Tab:** centres the text around the tab stop.
- **Right Tab:** right-aligns the text at the tab stop.
- **Decimal Tab:** aligns decimal numbers using the decimal point.

You can choose which tab stop to use by clicking on the tab selector, which is found to the left of the horizontal ruler.

Add tab stops

1 Select the paragraph or paragraphs that you want to add tab stops to. If you don't, the tabs will apply only to the current paragraph and any paragraphs you subsequently type beneath it.

2 Click the **tab selector** until the tab stop you wish to use appears. In this case, the decimal tab is shown.

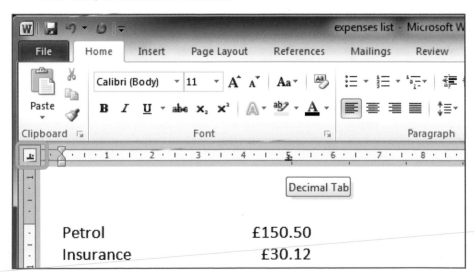

3 On the horizontal ruler, click where you want your tab stop to appear. You can add as many tab stops as you want. In this case there is a left-aligned tab at 0.75cm and a decimal tab at 5cm.

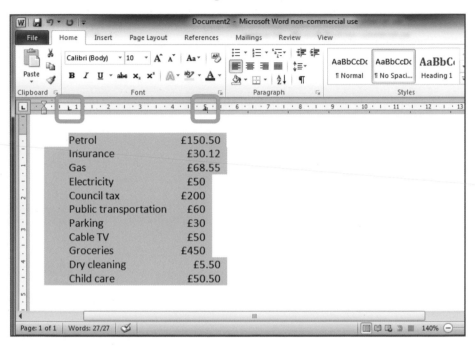

4 Now, in your paragraph, place your cursor before the text you wish to tab and press the **Tab** key. The text will jump to the next tab stop.

5 To get rid of a tab stop, simply drag it off the Ruler.

Tip

To help you find and delete section breaks in your text, click on the **Home** tab and, in the 'Paragraph' group, click on the **Show/Hide** symbol ¶. This will show section breaks and paragraph marks.

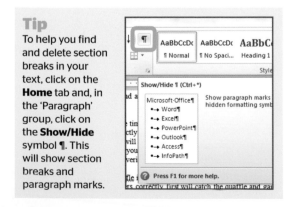

Indent text

Indenting the first line of every paragraph is a good way to visually separate paragraphs. You can also choose to indent every line of a paragraph or every line except the first line – known as a hanging indent. There are several ways to indent text in Word including using the horizontal ruler and the Indent commands on the 'Home' tab.

1 To create a first line indent or hanging indent, select the paragraph you want to indent. On the horizontal ruler, drag the First Line Indent marker to the position where you want the text to start.

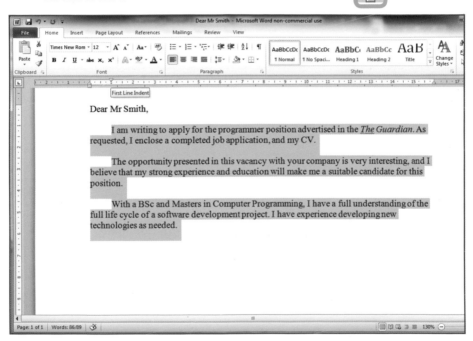

2 To create a hanging indent, drag the Hanging Indent marker to the position at which you want the indent to start.

Indent all of the lines in a paragraph

1 Select the text you wish to indent.

2 Click the **Home** tab.

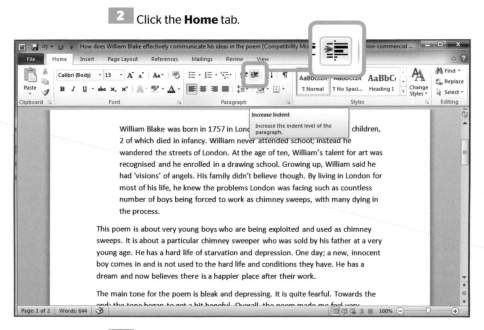

3 In the 'Paragraph' group, click **Increase Indent** to increase the indent by increments of 1.27cm.

4 Click **Decrease Indent** to reduce the indent by increments of 1.27cm.

Make a bulleted or numbered list

1 Type your list into the document, remembering to press **Enter** on your keyboard after each item so that they are all on separate lines.

2 Select all the text in your list.

3 On the **Home** tab, in the 'Paragraph' group, click the 'bullet point' **drop-down arrow**.

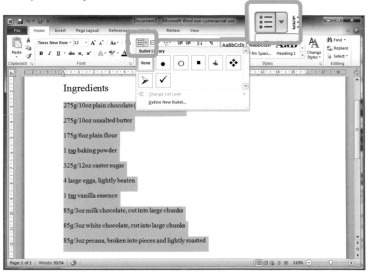

4 In the drop-down menu, preview the different bullet styles by holding your cursor over them.

5 Click to select your choice. The same principle applies to numbering your list with the numbering icon.

Work with text

Use the Format Painter

Word's Format Painter offers a quick way to copy the text or paragraph formatting for one area of the document and apply it to another in just a couple of clicks.

1 Select the text or paragraph that has the formatting you want to copy.

2 On the **Home** tab, in the 'Clipboard' group, click **Format Painter**. The pointer changes to a paintbrush icon.

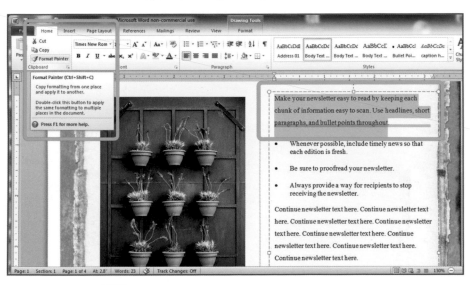

3 Select the text that you want to format.

Use drop caps

Often found in children's storybooks or the start of newspaper stories, drop caps are the large initial letters or words that appear at the start of a page or paragraph. Even if you're not writing fairy tales, drops caps are useful for adding style and drawing the reader's focus to certain areas of your document.

Add a drop cap

1 Highlight the letter or word at the start of a paragraph that you want to turn into a drop cap.

2 Click the **Insert** tab and, in the 'Text' group, click **Drop Cap**. A drop-down menu will appear.

3 Move your cursor over an option (in this case, 'Dropped') to see a live preview of the drop cap in your document.

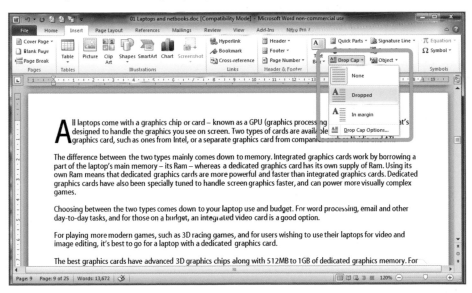

4 Click **Dropped** (or any other option) to apply it.

Modify a drop cap

Once you've created a drop cap, you can resize it by dragging on the lower right corner of the box that surrounds it. You can also use the 'Drop Cap Options' to specify how your drop cap should look:

1 Add a drop cap as described on page 57. From the drop-down menu click **Drop Cap Options...**.

2 In the dialog box that appears, you can select the following:

- **Font:** choose the font used for the drop cap. This won't change the paragraph's font and you can later change the drop cap's font by simply highlighting it and changing the font as you would with any text.
- **Lines to drop:** this determines the size of the drop cap – the more lines you choose, the larger the drop cap will be.
- **Distance from text:** this positions the drop cap relative to the paragraph text.

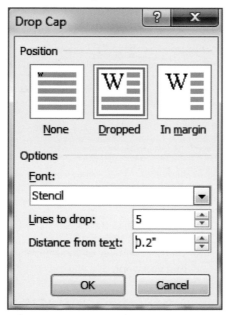

3 Click **OK** to apply.

Line and paragraph spacing

Line and paragraph spacing is a vital part of good page layout, ensuring your text is legible and comfortable to read. Line spacing refers to the amount of vertical space between the lines of text in a paragraph. Paragraph spacing determines the amount of space above or below a paragraph.

Line spacing – also known as leading – can either be measured in lines or points. So, for example, when text is double-spaced, the spacing is two lines high. Or you might have 10-point size text with a 12-point spacing.

Change line spacing

1 Select the text for which you want to change the line spacing.

2 Click the **Home** tab and, in the 'Paragraph' group, click **Line Spacing**.

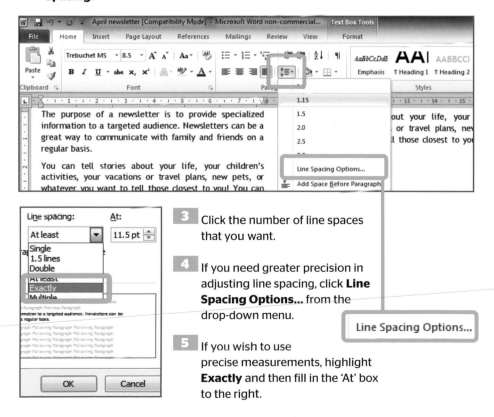

3 Click the number of line spaces that you want.

4 If you need greater precision in adjusting line spacing, click **Line Spacing Options...** from the drop-down menu.

5 If you wish to use precise measurements, highlight **Exactly** and then fill in the 'At' box to the right.

Change paragraph spacing for selected paragraphs

By default, paragraphs are separated by a blank line. As with line spacing, you can also adjust the spacing between each paragraph.

1 Select the text for which you want to change the line spacing.

2 On the **Home** tab, click **Line and Paragraph Spacing**.

3 Select **Add Space Before Paragraph** or **Remove Space After Paragraph** from the drop-down menu.

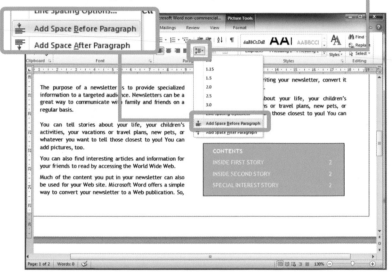

4 You can also select **Line Spacing Options...** on this menu to open the 'Paragraph' dialog box. Here, you can control exactly how much space there is before and after the paragraph.

Tip

In print, the general rule is to set the line spacing of text blocks at about 2 points above the size of the type: for example, 12-point text with 14 points of line spacing. If a document is to be read online, a more generous line spacing will compensate for the lower resolution of the computer screen.

5 If you've applied a style set (see pages 83–4) for line spacing, you can customise paragraph spacing using the paragraph spacing options. On the **Home** tab, in the 'Styles' group, click **Change Styles**. Point to 'Paragraph Spacing', and then click the option that you want.

BE CAREFUL!

Reducing line spacing will fit more lines of text on the page but as each line will sit more tightly on top of the next, it makes the text much harder to read.

Work with columns

By default, the text you enter into a Word document appears as one column across the entire page. Using more than one column can make your document more interesting and, with shorter line lengths, your text will be easier to read.

Add columns to a document

1 Select the text you want to format.

2 Click the **Page Layout** tab.

3 In the 'Page Setup' group, click **Columns**.

4 From the drop-down menu, select the number of columns you would like to insert.

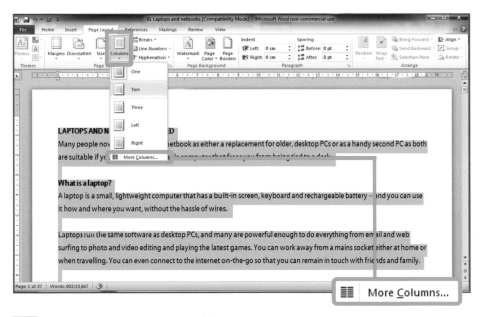

5 For precise control over the number of columns or their placement, select **More Columns...** from the drop-down menu. In the dialog box that appears adjust the settings to design your document.

Add column breaks

Once you've created columns in your document, the text will automatically flow from one column to the next. You may, however, want to control exactly where your text appears in a column. For example if you're creating a newsletter, you may need each column to start with a story heading. To do this, you can create column breaks.

1 Place the cursor where you want to add the break. In this case, in front of the words 'LAPTOPS TOUR'.

2 Click **Page Layout**.

3 In the 'Page Setup' group click **Breaks**.

4 From the list of break types select **Column**.

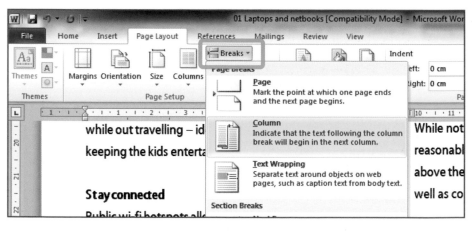

5 The text will move to the next column.

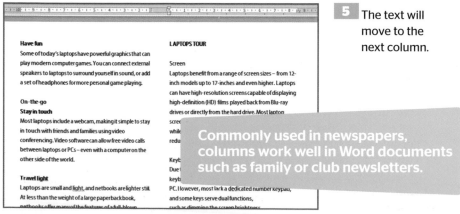

Commonly used in newspapers, columns work well in Word documents such as family or club newsletters.

Insert a page break

A page break divides your content and moves all the content after a page break divider to a new page. Word creates a page break automatically when your content fills a page, however to split the content in a different place, you can insert a manual page break.

1 Click in the content where you would like the new page to start.

2 On the **Insert** tab, In the 'Pages' group, click **Page Break**.

Control automatic page breaks

You can also specify where Word positions automatic page breaks so that paragraphs aren't split awkwardly:

1 Select the paragraph or paragraphs you want to affect.

2 On the **Page Layout** tab, in the 'Paragraph' group, click the 'More' **drop-down arrow** to open the 'Paragraph' dialog box. Click the **Line and Page Breaks** tab. Then select one of the following:

- **Widow/Orphan control:** to avoid widows and orphans.
- **Keep with next:** to prevent a page break between paragraphs.
- **Keep lines together:** to avoid a paragraph from being split in two.
- **Page break before:** to specify a page break before a paragraph.

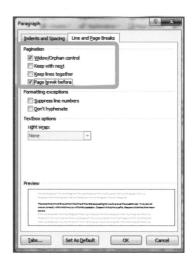

Remove a page break

While you can't remove the page breaks that Word has inserted into the document automatically, you can remove those that have been inserted manually:

1 On the **View** tab, in the 'Document Views' group, click **Draft**.

2 Select the page break by clicking in the margin next to the dotted line. Press the **Delete** key on your keyboard.

Jargon buster
Widow and orphan The last line of a paragraph by itself at the top of a page is known as a widow, while the first line of a paragraph by itself at the bottom of a page is known as an orphan.

Insert a section break

Sections breaks are useful when you need to vary the page layout of a long document. Dividing the document into sections allows you to format each section differently, for example changing headers and footers, page numbering and the number of columns.

Insert a section break

1 Place the cursor in your content where you want to add a section break.

2 On the **Page Layout** tab, in the 'Page Setup' group, click **Breaks**.

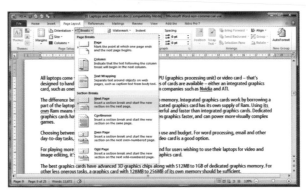

3 Select from one of four 'Section Breaks':
- **Next Page:** starts the new section on the next page.
- **Continuous:** starts the new section on the same page.
- **Even Page** and **Odd Page:** starts the new section on the next even-numbered or odd-numbered page in your document.

Delete a section break

1 Select the section break by dragging from its left edge all the way to the right edge.

2 Press the **Delete** key on your keyboard.

Work with the Clipboard

The Clipboard is a handy tool that lets you collect text, images and graphics from any Word document or Office program, and then paste them anywhere in your Word document.

It works with the standard Copy and Paste commands (see page 45). For example, you can copy a list from a PowerPoint presentation or a table from Excel or multiple items from your Word document – these will all be added to the Clipboard. You can then selectively paste these into your Word document at any time.

You can collect up to 24 items on the Clipboard, which are stored until you exit all your Office programs or you delete them from the Clipboard pane. If you copy a 25th item, the first item on the Clipboard is deleted.

Once you've quit all Office programs, only the last item that you copied stays on the Clipboard. Quitting all Office programs and restarting your computer will clear all items from the Clipboard.

Turn on the Clipboard

Unlike previous versions of Word, the Clipboard in Word 2010 isn't active automatically. You can turn it off or on with these steps:

1 Click the **Home** tab and, in the 'Clipboard' group, click the 'More' **drop-down arrow**.

2 The Clipboard pane will open to the right of your Word document.

3 You can reposition the Clipboard by clicking the down arrow at the top right of the pane and selecting **Move**. You can now drag the Clipboard to a position of choice.

Work with text

Cut and paste from the Clipboard

1 To cut or copy text (or a graphic) to the Clipboard, simply highlight it in your Word document, then on the **Home** tab in the 'Clipboard' group click **Cut** or **Copy**. The item will then appear in the Clipboard. Each entry has an icon that shows which Office program it was copied from, along with few lines of the copied text or a thumbnail of a copied graphic.

2 To paste an item from the Clipboard, first position the cursor where in your document you want it to appear.

3 In the Clipboard pane, click on the text or item that you want to paste into your document and select **Paste**.

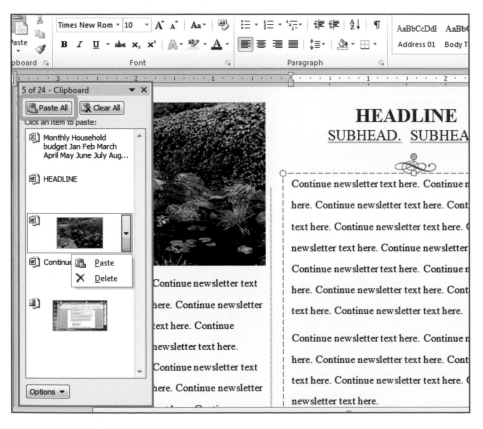

4 Alternatively, click **Paste All** to paste every item from the Clipboard into your document.

Remove items from the Clipboard

1 To remove a single item from the Clipboard, point the mouse at that item and click the downward-pointing triangle to the right of the item.

2 From the menu, click **Delete**.

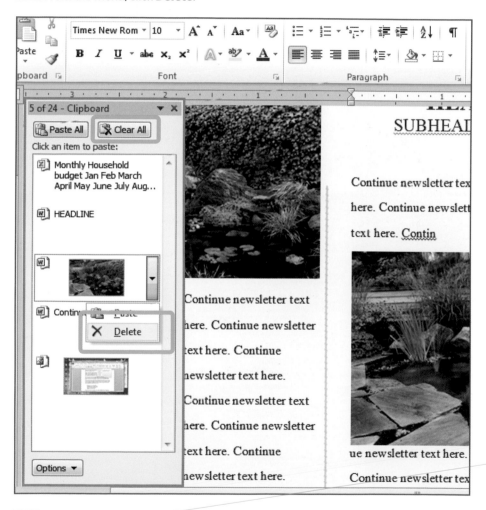

3 To remove all items on the Clipboard, click the **Clear All** button at the top of the Clipboard task pane.

Use the Paste commands

When you copy and paste text from another document or web page using the standard 'Cut' and 'Paste' commands, you often end up with odd formatting in your Word document. Fortunately, Word has a couple of tools that help avoid this irritating outcome – 'Paste Options' and 'Paste Special'.

Use Paste Options

When you paste text in Word, the 'Paste Options' icon automatically appears at the bottom of the pasted block of text. You can use these options to choose how the pasted text will be formatted. If you don't wish to make changes, you can carry on working, and the 'Paste Option' icon just disappears.

1 Paste the text into your Word document. The 'Paste Options' icon will appear at the end of the pasted text.

2 Click the 'Paste Options' **drop-down arrow**.

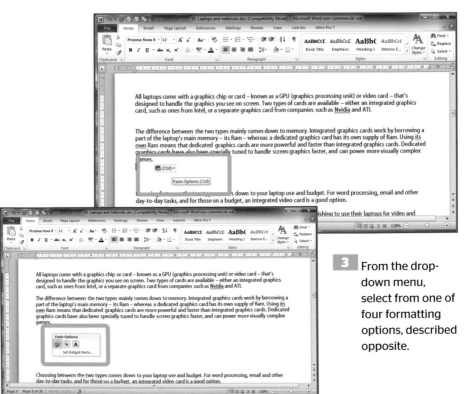

3 From the drop-down menu, select from one of four formatting options, described opposite.

You can choose from:

- **Keep Source Formatting:** keeps the original formatting from where the text was copied.
- **Merge Formatting:** changes the pasted text so that it matches the format of the text it's being pasted into.
- **Keep Text Only:** pastes as plain text with all formatting stripped out.

- **Set Default Paste…:** opens the 'Cut, copy, and paste' dialog box where you can customise Word's pasting.

Use Paste Special

Paste Special lets you convert the text or item you're pasting into another format before it is inserted into your document. For example, when copying text from a web page you may wish to remove unwanted HTML formatting before you paste it.

1 Copy the text you wish to insert into your Word document.

2 On the **Home** tab, in the 'Clipboard' group, click the 'Paste Options' **drop-down arrow**.

3 From the drop-down menu, select **Paste Special…**.

4 The 'Paste Special' dialog box appears. Choose the format the information should be pasted as and click **OK**.

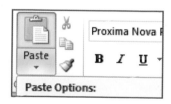

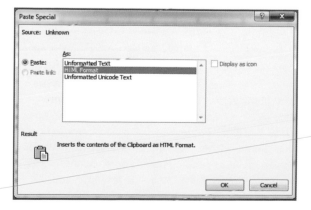

Check your spelling and grammar

Word has several tools to pick up poor grammar and spelling errors, including the 'Spelling and Grammar' tool, which can help you produce perfect documents.

Run a spelling and grammar check

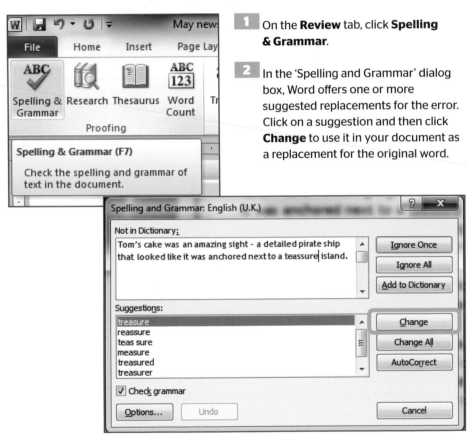

1 On the **Review** tab, click **Spelling & Grammar**.

2 In the 'Spelling and Grammar' dialog box, Word offers one or more suggested replacements for the error. Click on a suggestion and then click **Change** to use it in your document as a replacement for the original word.

3 If no suggestions are given, or the correct replacement is not shown, you can type in the correct spelling.

How to ignore errors

Word's spelling and grammar checker is not always accurate. Word may flag many words – such as people's names or place names – as potential spelling mistakes even if they're not. In this case, you can opt to leave such words as they were originally written by choosing one of the options on the opposite page.

- **Ignore Once:** skips this instance of the word without changing it.
- **Ignore All:** skips the word without changing it, and additionally it skips all subsequent instances of this word that appear in the document.
- **Add to Dictionary:** click this to add the word to the dictionary so that it will never be flagged as a spelling error in future documents.

For potential grammar errors flagged by Word in a document you are working on, you can choose from the following:

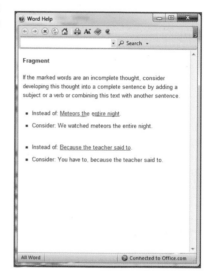

- **Ignore Once:** skips the potential error without changing it.
- **Ignore Rule:** skips the potential error along with all other instances that relate to this grammar rule.
- **Next Sentence:** skips the sentence without changing it, but leaves it marked as an error. This means it will be flagged again on subsequent spelling and grammar checks.

If you're not sure if something Word has flagged is actually a grammar error, click **Explain...** to see why Word thinks it's wrong. This will help you decide if it needs to be rewritten.

Check spelling and grammar automatically

You may not need to run a separate spelling and grammar check as Word can automatically check your document for both spelling and grammar errors as you type. Potential mistakes are underlined by wavy, coloured lines with a red line indicating a misspelled word, green a grammar mistake and blue a contextual spelling error.

A contextual spelling error is when a correctly spelled word is used in the wrong context. For example, if the text reads 'weather that is true or not', weather is a contextual spelling error because it should read 'whether'. Weather is accurately spelled, but used incorrectly in this instance.

Use the spell checker to fix automatically flagged errors

1 Right click the underlined word.

2 From the pop-up menu that appears, click on the correct spelling of the word from the listed suggestions.

3 The word will be corrected in your document.

You can also choose to Ignore an underlined word, add it to the dictionary, or go to the 'Spelling' dialog box for more options.

Use the grammar checker

1 Right click the underlined word or phrase.

2 From the pop-up menu, click on the correct phrase from the listed suggestions.

3 The phrase will be corrected in your document.

You can also choose to ignore an underlined phrase, go to the 'Grammar' dialog box, or click **About This Sentence** for information about the grammar rule.

Change automatic spelling and grammar check settings

If you prefer Word not to flag spelling and grammar problems as you type, you can turn off the automatic spelling and grammar checker or adjust the settings to make it more useful and relevant to your text.

1 Click the **File** tab to go to the Backstage view.

2 Click on **Options**, then select **Proofing**.

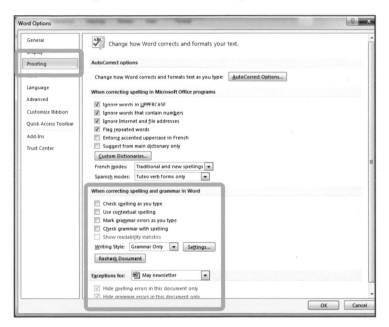

3 In this dialog box choose from the following options:

- To stop Word automatically checking spelling, untick **Check spelling as you type**.
- To check for contextual spelling errors, tick the **Use contextual spelling** box.
- To stop grammar errors from being marked, untick **Mark grammar errors as you type**.
- If you want to stop Word from automatically checking just this document then tick the **Hide spelling errors in this document only** and **Hide grammar errors in this document only** boxes.

4 Click **OK**.

Change the spell check language

By default Word will spell check your text using a US English dictionary, but you can change the language used for spell checking.

1 Select the text you want to check.

2 On the **Review** tab, in the 'Language' group, click **Language**.

3 Click **Set Proofing Language...**.

4 In the 'Language' dialog box, select the language you want to use for spell checking – for example, **English (U.K.)**.

5 Click **OK**. When you run a spell check, it will check in the language you have selected.

Count the number of words

As you type in a document, Word automatically counts the number of words and displays the amount on the Status bar at the bottom of the window. If you can't see this, make sure **word count** is selected on the Status bar (see pages 16–17).

Sometimes, however, you may want to count the number of words in just a selected piece of text or in text boxes.

Count words in a selection

Selections don't need to be adjacent in order to count them. Simply select the first section, and then hold down the **Ctrl** key and select the other sections.

1 Select the text that you want to count.

2 The Status bar will show the number of words in the selection. For example, 56/1,124 means that the selection accounts for 56 words of the 1,124 total number of words in the document.

For more information about your text or to include text in footnotes, endnotes and text boxes throughout your document use the **Review** tab.

1 On the **Review** tab, in the 'Proofing' group, click **Word Count**.

2 In the 'Word Count' dialog box, select the **Include textboxes, footnotes and endnotes check box**.

3 The 'Word Count' dialog box shows the number of pages, paragraphs and lines in your document, along with the number of characters.

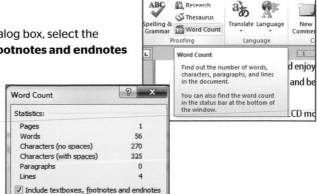

Use Find and Replace

Once you've created a Word document, you may decide to replace a certain word or phrase used in the text. Searching for every instance of that word throughout a long document is not only tedious, there's a risk you may overlook one. Word's Find and Replace feature can do the hard work for you. Here's how:

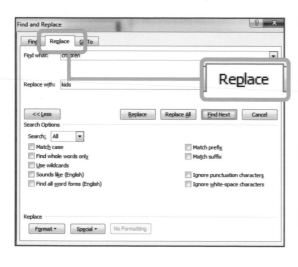

1 On the **Home** tab, in the 'Editing' group, click **Replace**.

2 The 'Find and Replace' dialog box appears. Select the **Replace** tab.

3 In the 'Find what' box, type the text you want to find.

4 In the 'Replace with' box, type the text you want to replace it with.

5 In 'Search Options', click the 'Search' **drop-down arrow** and select **All**, **Up** or **Down** so Word knows which part of the document to use for the search and replace text.

6 If you want to manually replace each word or phrase, click **Find Next** and when the text is found, click **Replace**. Word replaces the found text, highlighted onscreen, with the text typed in the 'Replace with' box. It then immediately searches for the next instance of the text. Repeat this step until the entire document has been searched.

7 Alternatively, to get Word to automatically search for and replace each instance of the word or phrase, click **Replace All** after Step 5.

As Word starts its search based on where your cursor is positioned in the document, place it at the beginning of your text to ensure a thorough search.

Use Find and Replace to replace text formatting

'Find and Replace' can also be used to change styles – text formatting – that you have applied to text. You might, for example, want to replace all instances of a particular font with a new font.

1 On the **Home** tab, in the 'Editing' group, click **Replace**.

2 The 'Find and Replace' dialog box appears. Click **More** on the bottom left of the dialog box.

3 Click **Format**, and from the pop-up choose the formats you want to change. In this case, choose **Font**.

4 In the 'Find Font' dialog box, select the font you wish to change. Then click **OK**.

5 Click in the 'Replace with' box.

6 Click **Format** and from the pop up dialog box choose the formats you wish to change to. In this case, choose **Font** and then in the 'Find Font' dialog box select the font you wish to change to. Then click **OK**.

7 Click the **Find** tab.

8 Click **Reading Highlight** and select **Highlight All**.

9 Click the **Replace** tab. Click **Replace All**. All highlighted instances of the text will then be changed to the new format.

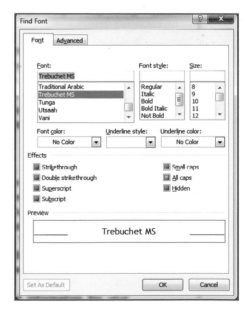

Work with AutoFormat

You can use Word's AutoFormat feature to help create a well-designed document that's easy to read. You can automatically format text either as you type or after you've written it using a predefined list of options. It may, for example, automatically turn all website and email address into hyperlinks, replace hyphens with dashes, and single quote marks with proper curly quote marks.

By default, Word will autoformat your text as you type, but if you disagree with the changes it makes, you can turn off certain AutoFormat options or turn it off completely.

Turn off 'AutoFormat As You Type' options

1 With Word open, click the **File** tab and in the left-hand pane click **Options**.

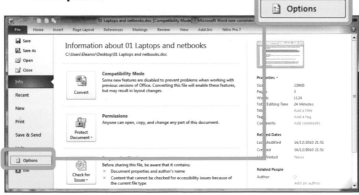

2 Click **Proofing**, and then click **AutoCorrect Options...**.

AutoCorrect Options...

Jargon buster

Hyperlink A hyperlink is coloured and underlined text or an image that you click to open a file, a web page, another location in the document or email program.

3 Click the **AutoFormat As You Type** tab.

4 Select or clear the check boxes for the options that you want to enable or disable under 'Replace as you type', 'Apply as you type' and 'Automatically as you type'. After you do this, you can format these items manually. To effectively turn off Word's AutoFormatting, clear all the check boxes.

5 Click **OK** twice.

Access the AutoFormat button

Even if you've turned off AutoFormat As You Type, you can still apply automatic formatting to all, or just a selection, of the text in your document using the AutoFormat command. Although this isn't available by default on Word 2010's menus, you can add it to the Ribbon or, for even quicker access, to the Quick Access Toolbar. Here's how:

1 On the **File** tab click **Options**.

2 Click **Quick Access Toolbar** in the left-hand pane.

3 Under 'Choose commands from' click the arrow next to 'Popular Commands' and select **All Commands** from the drop-down menu.

4 Select one of the AutoFormat commands:
- **AutoFormat Now:** to apply formatting to an entire document,
- **AutoFormat Options…:** to show the 'AutoFormat' dialog box before applying the format.

5 Click **Add** and then click **OK**. The AutoFormat button will now appear in the Quick Access Toolbar.

6 To use the AutoFormat command, simply select the text you wish to apply autoformatting to, and then click the AutoFormat icon on the Quick Access Toolbar. Your text will be changed according to the default autoformatting options or those you've specified.

Select a list of AutoFormat options

To customise the list of automatic format options that apply when you click the **AutoFormat** button, follow these steps:

1 With Word open, click the **File** tab.

2 Select **Options** from the left-hand pane.

3 Click **Proofing**, and then click **AutoCorrect Options**.

4 In the 'AutoCorrect' pop-up window, click **AutoFormat**.

5 Select or clear the check boxes for the options you want to enable or disable under 'Apply', 'Replace', 'Preserve' and 'Always AutoFormat' groups.

6 Click **OK** twice. Word will now autoformat the selected text using only the features that you've chosen.

Hide or show text

Word has an interesting feature that lets you hide any text in the document so that it's not visible – useful if you want to hide confidential or sensitive information. When you hide text, the space it takes up is also removed so it's as if the text never existed. However, hiding text is not the same as deleting text. Although there's no sign of the text, it's still there in the document.

Hide text

1 Select the text you want to hide.

2 On the **Home** tab, click the small downwards pointing arrow at the bottom right of the 'Font' group to launch the 'Font' dialog box.

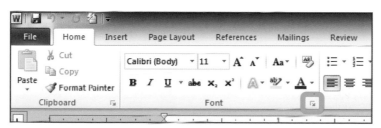

3 Click the **Hidden** check box in the 'Effects' section.

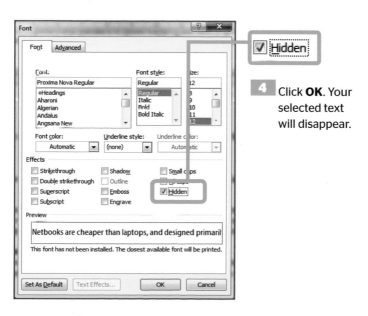

4 Click **OK**. Your selected text will disappear.

Show text

To show all the hidden text in your document:

1 Select all the text in your document.

2 On the **Home** tab, click the small downwards pointing arrow at the bottom right of the 'Font' group to launch the 'Font' dialog box.

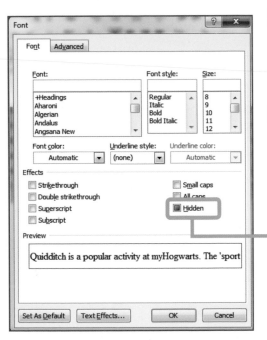

3 The 'Hidden' check box won't have a check mark in it (because your selection includes hidden and non-hidden text), but it will be filled with a colour.

4 Click the check box once. It will change it into a check mark meaning all the text in the document is hidden. Click it again to remove the check mark and reveal all hidden text.

☑ <u>H</u>idden

If you choose to hide sensitive information as described above, remember that others can use the same steps to reveal your text. You will need to protect your document so that no one can change these formats (see page 150).

Work with Styles and Themes

Styles and Themes are useful features that can help you to quickly create professional Word 2010 documents. Applied to selected text with just one click, a Style is a combination of text formats that includes font name, font size, colour, paragraph alignment and spacing. A Theme is a set of colours, fonts and effects that can be applied to the entire document with just one click to give it a consistent look.

Character and paragraph styles

On the **Home** tab in the 'Styles' group, Word includes a number of built-in styles designed to complement each other and therefore make it easier for you to format a document. For example, the Heading 2 is designed to look subordinate to the Heading 1, so works well as a subhead or crosshead. Other built-in styles include 'Emphasis' and 'List Paragraph'.

You can apply a style by selecting it from the gallery on the **Home** tab. Click the down arrow to see more styles. Alternatively, click the small downwards-pointing arrow at the bottom right corner of the group. This launches the 'Styles' dialog box, which provides more information about the styles.

Character styles are marked with a character symbol: a. They may include all the formatting characteristics that can be applied to text, such as font name, size, colour, bold, italic, underline, borders and shading.

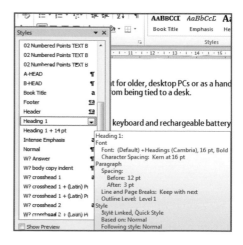

Paragraph styles are marked by a paragraph symbol ¶ and include everything that a character style contains, but may also control all aspects of a paragraph's appearance, such as text alignment, tab stops, line spacing and borders.

Some styles – known as linked styles – can be applied to either a character or a paragraph. These are marked with both a paragraph symbol and a character symbol: ¶a .

Apply a style

1 Select the text that you want to format.

2 On the **Home** tab, in the 'Styles' group move your cursor over each style to see a live preview.

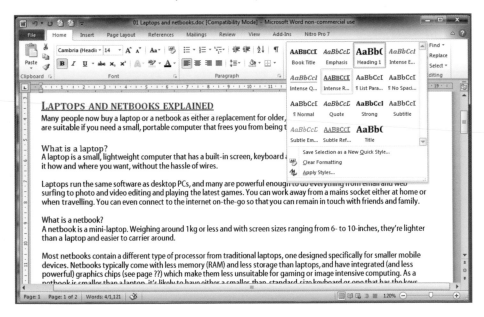

3 Click the 'More' **drop-down arrow** to see Word's additional styles.

4 Click a style and your selected text will be formatted in that style.

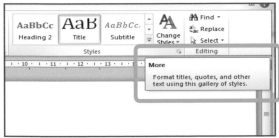

Another advantage of using Word's built-in styles (Heading 1, Heading 2, and so on) is that Word can generate a table of contents for your document automatically. This is a real timesaver.

Apply a Quick Style Set

Style Sets include a mix of title, heading and paragraph styles. They provide a fast way to format your document in one go rather than formatting individual lines of text and paragraphs.

1 On the **Home** tab and in the 'Styles' group, click **Change Styles**.

2 From the drop-down menu, select **Style Set**.

3 Click a Style Set – in this case, **Formal** – and your document will change accordingly.

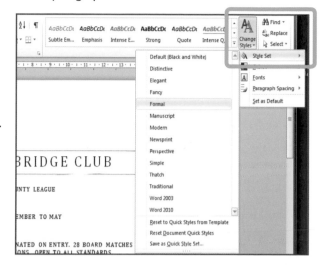

Choose a theme

Word comes with several built-in themes including the default Office theme. You can also download more themes from Microsoft Office Online as well as create and save your own themes. You choose a theme from the themes gallery found on the 'Page Layout' tab in the 'Themes' group.

1 On the **Page Layout** tab, click **Themes**.

2 Move your cursor over a theme to see a live preview of it.

3 Click on a theme to apply it.

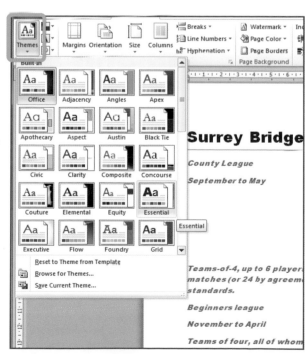

Modify a theme

You may find a theme in which you like the fonts and effects but you'd prefer to use different colours. Word lets you tweak a theme's colours, fonts and effects to create your own custom themes.

1 To change the theme colours, on the **Page Layout** tab click **Theme Colors**.

2 On the drop-down menu, move your cursor over the colour sets to see a live preview.

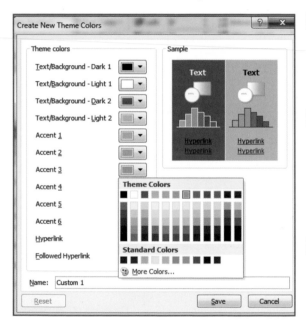

3 Click a set of **Theme Colors**, or select **Create New Theme Colors...** to adjust each colour separately.

4 To change the theme fonts, on the **Page Layout** tab click **Theme Fonts**. On the drop-down menu, move your cursor over the font sets to see a live preview.

5 Click a set of **Theme Fonts**, or select **Create New Theme Fonts** to choose each font separately.

6 To change the theme effects, on the **Page Layout** tab click **Theme Effects**.

7 On the drop-down menu, move your cursor over the effects sets to see a live preview. Click a set of **Theme Effects**.

Tip

You can choose to save a customised theme so you can use it in other documents. On the **Page Layout** tab, click **Themes** and select **Select Save Current Theme**. Give your theme a name and click **Save**.

Add hyperlinks

Word automatically creates a hyperlink when you type a web or email address, unless you've turned off this option in AutoFormatting (see page 78). Even if you have, you can still create hyperlinks manually.

Add a hyperlink

1 Select and then right click the text or image you want to make a hyperlink.

2 From the pop-up menu click **Hyperlink...**.

Tip
You can also get to the Insert Hyperlink dialog box by clicking **Hyperlink** on the **Insert** tab.

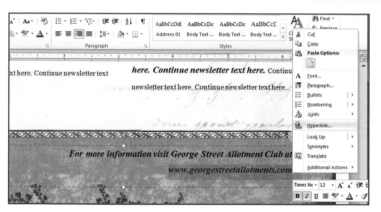

3 The 'Insert Hyperlink' dialog box opens. If you selected text, it appears in the 'Text to display' field at the top. To use different text here, simply highlight the text and rewrite (see TIP, right).

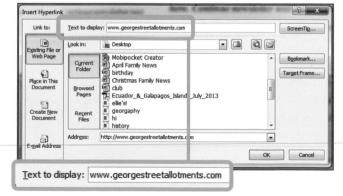

4 In the 'Address' field at the bottom, type the address that you want to use.

5 Click **OK**. The text or image you selected will now be a hyperlink.

Make an email address a hyperlink

1 Select and then right click the text or image you want to use and from the pop-up menu select **Hyperlink...**.

2 From the left side of the 'Insert Hyperlink' dialog box, click the **Email Address** button.

3 In the 'E-mail Address' field, type the email address you want to connect to. Click **OK**.

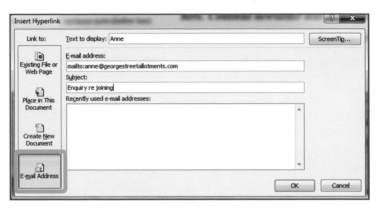

Delete a hyperlink

1 Right click the text or image that is the hyperlink you wish to remove.

2 From the pop-up menu, click **Remove Hyperlink**.

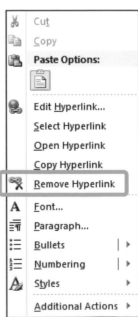

Tip

Hyperlinks are made up of two parts: the **address** of the web page, email address, or other location that they link to, and the **display** text (or image). Often, the display text is the same as the address, but you can make them different. For example, you can select the word **Which?** as the display text for the hyperlink that takes you to **www.which.co.uk** when clicked on.

Photos and graphics

By reading and following all the steps in this chapter, you will get to grips with:

- Adding images to your documents
- Working with shapes and tables
- Inserting text boxes and WordArt

Add images to a document

Add interest to your documents with a picture: useful for creating family or club newsletters, for example. You can add a picture from a file – such as a photo you've taken – or copy one from a web page or use one of Word's many clip art images. You can change how a picture or clip art is positioned in relation to text within a document by using the 'Position' and 'Wrap Text' commands.

Jargon buster
Clip art Ready-made artwork that is included with your Office software or can be downloaded from the web for use in your documents and presentations. Clip art includes both subject-related illustrations and elements such as horizontal lines, symbols, bullets and backgrounds.

Add clip art

1 Place your cursor in the document where you wish to insert the clip art. On the **Insert** tab, in the 'Illustrations' group, click **Clip Art**.

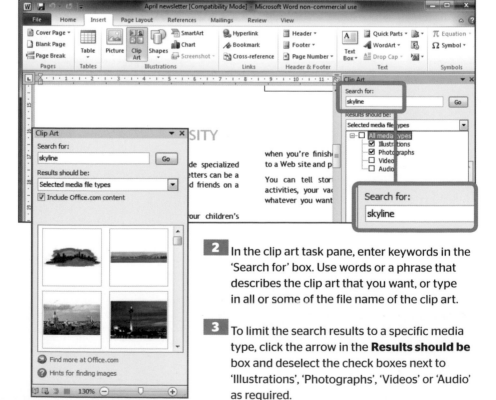

2 In the clip art task pane, enter keywords in the 'Search for' box. Use words or a phrase that describes the clip art that you want, or type in all or some of the file name of the clip art.

3 To limit the search results to a specific media type, click the arrow in the **Results should be** box and deselect the check boxes next to 'Illustrations', 'Photographs', 'Videos' or 'Audio' as required.

4 To expand your search to include clip art on the web, click the **Include Office.com** content check box. Otherwise the search will be limited to only your computer hard drive. Click **Go**.

5 In the list of results, click the clip art to insert it. It will appear in your document.

Insert a picture from a file

1 Place your cursor in the document where you wish the image to be eventually positioned.

2 On the **Insert** tab, click **Picture** from the 'Illustrations' group. The 'Insert Picture' dialog box appears.

3 Choose the picture file you want and click **Insert** to place it in your document.

Insert a picture from a web page

You can drag a picture from a web page into your open Word document. However, avoid dragging a picture that has a link to another web page. If you do, it will be appear in your document as a link (a line of text giving the address of the linked web page) rather than the image itself.

BE CAREFUL!
While it's easy to copy and paste pictures and even video from websites, be sure to check the copyright of these items before you do. Check the website for copyright notices. Copyright is owned by the person who created the picture or video. It's illegal to copy and use anything protected by copyright without the permission of the copyright owner.

Resize clip art or a picture

1 Select the clip art or picture you've placed in the document.

2 Drag a sizing handle away from or toward the centre of the image. To keep the image's proportions, press and hold **Shift** while you drag the sizing handle.

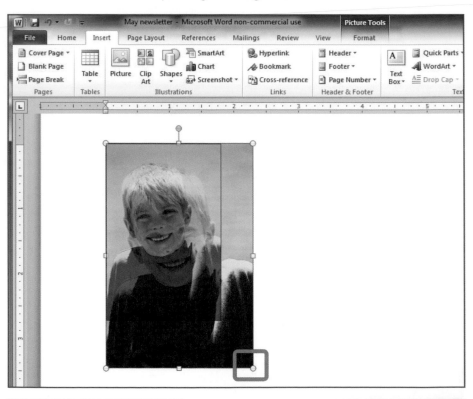

Jargon buster

Sizing handles When you click an object, such as a shape, image or clip art, in Word, a border with little white squares and circles will appear around it. These squares and circles are the sizing handles. You click on the squares to change the height or width, while the circles are used to make the whole object smaller or bigger.

To resize a picture to an exact height and width, click the picture and on the **Format** tab in the 'Size' group, enter the measurements that you want in the 'Height' and 'Width' boxes.

Position images

By default, Word inserts images as inline pictures. This means they keep their position relative to the text where they were inserted. This can make it difficult to move an image exactly where you want. You can solve this problem with the text wrapping setting.

1 Select the image.

2 On the **Format** tab, click **Position**.

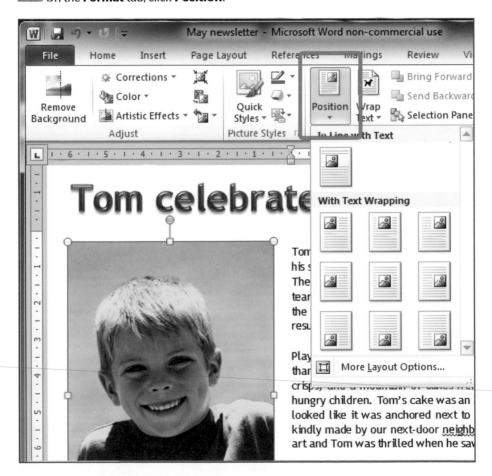

3 From the drop-down menu, choose an image position.

4 The image will move to the position you've selected, and text wrapping will automatically be applied to it.

Wrap text around an image

1 Select the image.

2 On the **Format** tab, click **Wrap Text**. Choose a text wrap option. The text will adjust based on the option you've chosen.

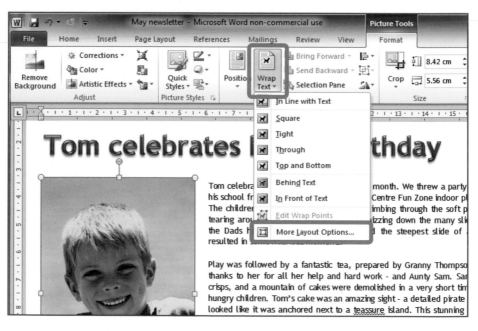

3 For more control on how text wraps around your image, click **More Layout Options...** from the menu. In the 'Advanced Layout' dialog box that appears, you can make more precise adjustments such as specifying the exact size of the text wrap around an image – with measurements for both top and bottom as well as left and right.

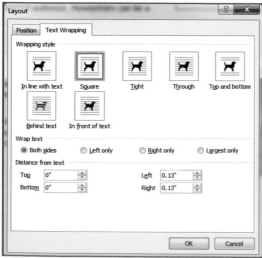

Work with irregular shapes

Word's default text wrap settings are great for working with square or rectangular shaped images. But when you place an irregularly shaped image in your document, text may wrap haphazardly around the image. So, use Word's 'Edit Wrap Points' tool to fine-tune the text wrap. Wrap points are small black square handles, similar to the resize handles. Moving or removing or adding wrap points affects the shape of the flow of text around your image.

Edit wrap points

1 Select the picture.

2 On the **Format** tab, click **Wrap Text** in the 'Arrange' group. Select **Edit Wrap Points** from the drop-down list.

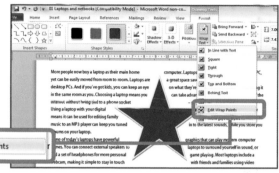

3 A dashed red line will appear around your picture. Click and drag on the handles to adjust the edge of the text wrap. The text will adjust accordingly around your image.

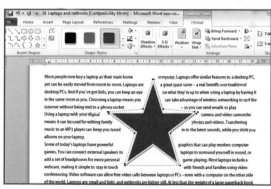

4 To fine-tune the text wrap you can create your own wrap points. Simply click anywhere on the red outline where you want the new wrap point. You can then drag the new point to a new position.

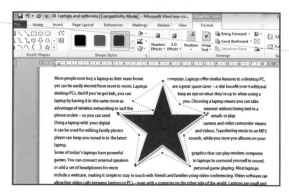

5 To delete a wrap point, hold down **Ctrl** and click the wrap point you want to remove.

Edit images

Once you've positioned pictures in your document, you can make changes to them using Word's picture tools. There are lots of ways to adjust your images including changing their shape, cropping or compressing pictures, and adding borders and artistic effects.

Crop an image

1 Select the image you want to crop.

2 On the **Format** tab, in the 'Size' group, click **Crop**.

Jargon buster

Crop A photo-editing term that means removing unwanted areas from a photo.

3 Black cropping handles appear around your picture – similar to those used to resize an image. Click and drag a handle to crop an image. Clicking on the corner handles simultaneously also crops the image horizontally and vertically.

4 When you've finished, click **Crop** to deselect the crop tool.

Crop an image to a shape

Word's crop tool not only removes unwanted areas of an image but can also be used to crop to a shape. Much like cookie cutters, you can choose a shape to stamp out of your image.

1 Select the image you want to work with.

2 On the **Format** tab, click on the down arrow below 'Crop' and select **Crop to Shape**.

3 From the drop-down menu, choose a shape. The image will take the shape that you have selected.

Remove an image background

1 Click on the image.

2 On the **Format** tab, click **Remove Background**.

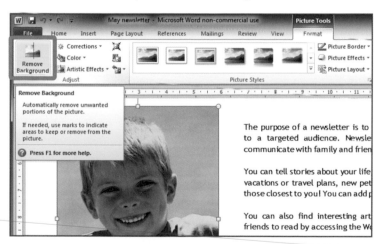

3 Word makes a guess which part of the image is the background. It colours this area pink and draws a box with selection handles around the part of the image that will remain.

4 Make sure all of the image you wish to keep is within the box by adjusting the selection handles.

5 To change the areas selected as background use the 'Mark Areas to Keep' and 'Mark Areas to Remove' commands:

To show which parts of the image that you want to keep, click **Mark Areas to Keep**. The cursor changes into a pencil. Click and drag to draw a line in that region of the image.

If you want to remove part of the background but it hasn't been automatically been selected, click **Mark Areas to Remove**. The cursor changes into a pencil. Click and drag to draw a line in that region of the image.

6 When you've made your adjustments, Word will readjust the image automatically.

7 Click **Keep Changes**. All of the pink areas will be removed from the image.

Tip

If you change your mind about an area you've marked with a line when removing a picture background, either to keep or to remove it, click **Delete Mark** and then click the line to change it.

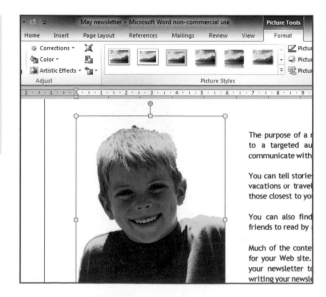

Rotate an image

1 Click the picture that you want to rotate.

2 For manual rotation, click on the rotation handle (the green circle) at the top of the picture, and simply drag it in the direction that you want to rotate the shape.

3 For more control over the rotation, click **Rotate** on the **Format** tab.

4 Click **More Rotation Options**.

5 In the 'Layout' dialog box, click the **Size** tab, and enter the angle that you want to rotate the object in the 'Rotation' box. Using a negative number will rotate the picture anticlockwise.

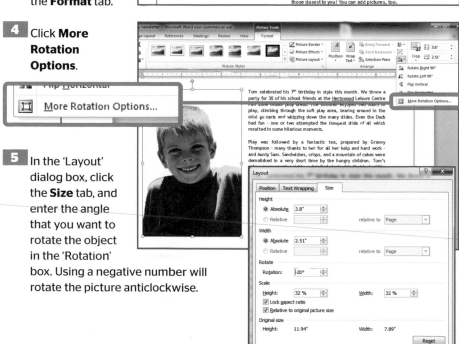

Flip a picture

When you flip a picture, you create a reverse image.

1 Click the picture that you want to flip.

2 On the **Format** tab, in the 'Arrange' group, click the **Rotate** icon and then to reverse the picture vertically, click **Flip Vertical**. Alternatively, to reverse the picture horizontally, click **Flip Horizontal**.

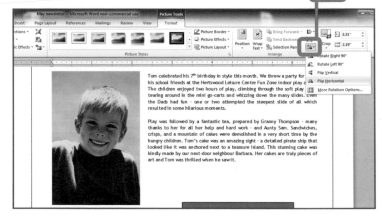

Add a border to an image

1 Select the image.

2 On the **Format** tab, click **Picture Border**.

3 From the drop-down menu, select a colour, weight (thickness of the border), and a line style.

Change image brightness and contrast

1 Select the image. On the **Format** tab in the 'Adjust' group, click **Corrections**. A drop-down menu will appear.

2 To sharpen or soften your picture, move your cursor over the 'Sharpen' and 'Soften' presets to see a live preview of how your image will look with the preset applied.

3 Click on a preset to apply it.

4 To adjust the brightness, move your cursor over the 'Brightness' and 'Contrast' presets to see a live preview of how your image will look with the preset applied.

5 Click on a preset to apply it.

Tip

For greater control over sharpness, brightness and contrast, click **Picture Corrections Options** from the 'Corrections' drop-down menu to refine the settings.

Adjust image colour

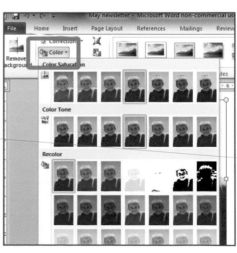

1 Select the image. On the **Format** tab, click **Color**. A drop-down menu will appear.

2 Here you can choose a preset for each of the following options:

- **Color Saturation:** changes the strength of colours in the image.
- **Color Tone:** affects colour 'temperature' – from cool to warm.
- **Recolor:** changes the overall colour of the image. This option can be used to turn an image into black and white or give it a different colour.

Apply an artistic effect

1 Select the picture. On the **Format** tab, click **Artistic Effects**.

2 On the drop-down menu, move your cursor over a preset to see a live preview.

3 Click on a preset to apply it.

4 You can adjust the settings for an effect by clicking **Artistic Effects** and then selecting **Artistic Effect Options…**.

Apply a picture style

1 Select the picture.

2 On the **Format** tab, in the 'Picture Styles' group, click the 'More' **drop-down arrow** to show all available picture styles.

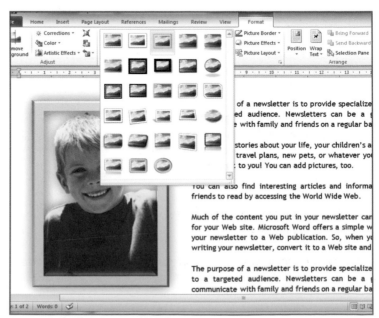

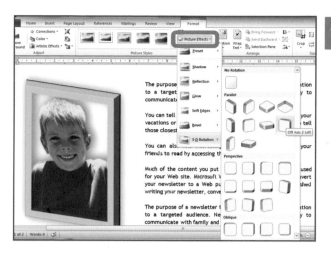

3 Move your cursor over a picture style to see a live preview of the style in your document.

4 Click on the style to apply it.

5 To fine-tune your chosen picture style, click **Picture Effects** to see the 'Effects' drop-down menu.

Compress pictures

Using lots of large, high-resolution pictures can have a big impact on the file size of your Word document, which may make it difficult to share with others via email. Fortunately, you can reduce the file size of your document by lowering image resolution, applying compression and deleting unwanted areas such as cropped parts of an image.

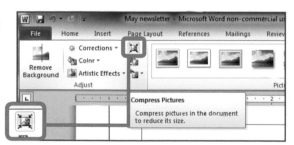

1 Select the picture.

2 On the **Format** tab, in the 'Adjust' group, click **Compress Pictures**.

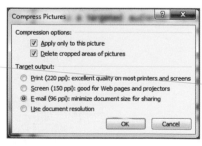

3 In the dialog box that appears, choose a 'Target output'. If you're emailing your document, you may want to select **Email**, which produces the smallest file size.

4 Tick the box next to **Delete cropped areas of pictures**.

5 You can choose whether to apply these settings to this picture only or to all pictures in the document. Tick the **Apply only to this picture** box to apply these settings to just the image selected. Click **OK**.

Make images transparent

You can use transparency on the images in your Word document in order to create clever effects. For example, you can create custom stationery by using a partially transparent image as a background, or by making just part of an image transparent in a document, any text that's layered on top can be read more clearly.

Apply transparency to an image

To make an entire image transparent or partially transparent, it must first be inserted into a shape.

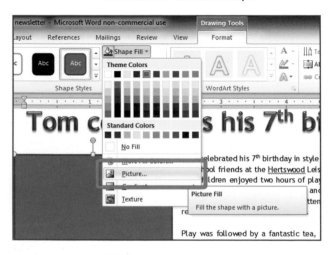

1 Insert a shape, such as a rectangle, into your document.

2 With the shape selected, on the **Format** tab, in the 'Shape Styles' group, click **Shape Fill**.

3 From the 'Shape Fill' drop-down menu, click **Picture...**.

4 In the 'Insert Picture' dialog box, choose a picture to insert and click **Insert**.

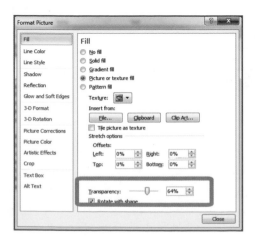

5 On the **Format** tab, in the 'Shape Styles' group, click the 'More' **drop-down arrow** to launch the 'Format Picture' dialog box.

6 Click **Fill** in the left-hand pane.

7 Move the **Transparency** slider or adjust the percentage value to make the picture more transparent.

8 Click **Close** to quit the 'Format Picture' dialog box.

Apply transparency to part of an image

You can also choose to make part of your picture transparent.
However, this applies to only a single colour in your picture – so it
only works on areas of strong colour. Even areas that appear to be
a single colour, such as a blue sky, may in fact consist of many slight
colour variations, making it difficult to use this transparency effect.

1 Insert a picture into your Word document (see pages 90–1)
and select it.

2 On the **Format** tab, in the 'Adjust' group, click **Color**.

3 Click **Set Transparent Color**.

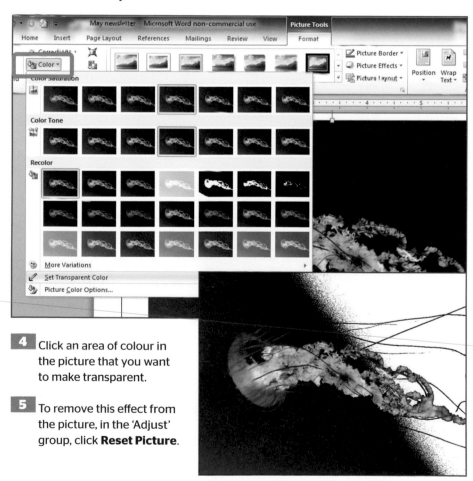

4 Click an area of colour in
the picture that you want
to make transparent.

5 To remove this effect from
the picture, in the 'Adjust'
group, click **Reset Picture**.

Work with shapes

Using shapes such as arrows, lines, squares, stars, flowchart shapes and banners not only adds visual appeal to your document, they can help make your text more legible and bring a message to life.

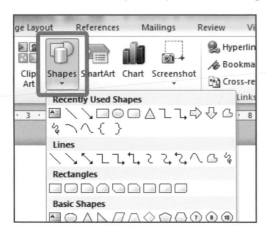

Add a shape

1 On the **Insert** tab, in the 'Illustrations' group, click **Shapes**.

2 Click on the shape that you want.

3 Click anywhere in your document, and then drag to place the shape at the size you want.

4 Release the mouse button.

Move a shape

1 Click on the shape.

2 Hover the cursor over one of the box's edges until it changes into a cross with arrows on each end.

3 Click and drag the shape to the desired location on the page.

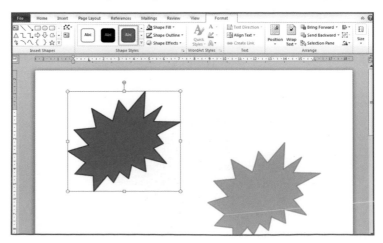

Resize or rotate a shape

1 Click on the shape to select it.

2 Click and drag one of the sizing handles on the corners and sides of the text box until it is the desired size.

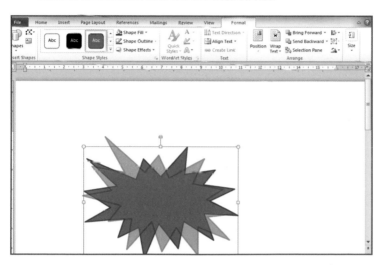

3 Drag the green circle to rotate the shape (see also page 111).

Flip a shape

1 Click the shape that you want to flip.

2 On the **Format** tab, in the 'Arrange' group, click the **Rotate** icon and then, to flip the object vertically, click **Flip Vertical**. Alternatively, to flip the object horizontally, click **Flip Horizontal**.

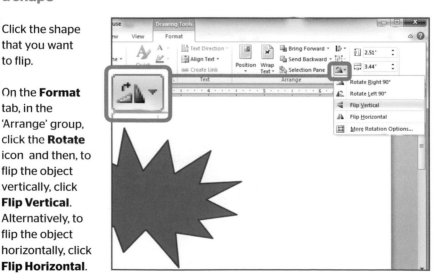

Change shape style

1 Select the shape.

2 On the **Format** tab, click the 'More' **drop-down arrow** in the 'Shape Styles' group to show further style options.

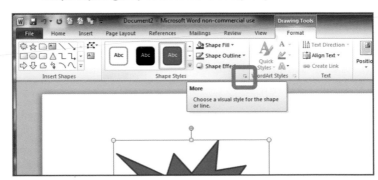

3 Move your cursor over a style to see a live preview in your document.

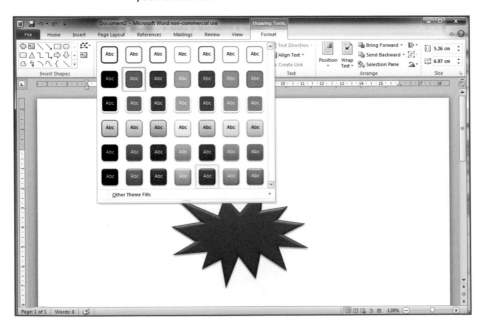

4 Select a style.

Fill with colour

1 Select the shape.

2 On the **Format** tab, click **Shape Fill**.

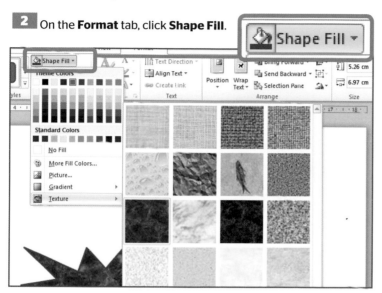

3 From the drop-down list, select either **a colour**, **No Fill** or **More Fill Colors...** for custom colour. You can also add a picture, gradient or texture to the shape.

4 To adjust the transparency of the shape's fill, click **More Fill Colors...**.

5 At the bottom of the 'Colors' dialog box, move the **Transparency slider**, or enter a number in the box next to the slider. You can adjust the percentage of transparency from 0% (fully opaque, the default setting) to 100% (fully transparent).

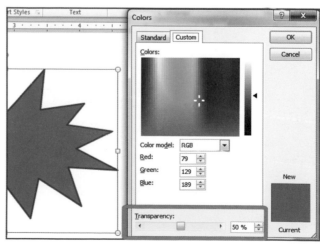

Change the shape outline

1 Select the shape.

2 On the **Format** tab, click **Shape Outline**.

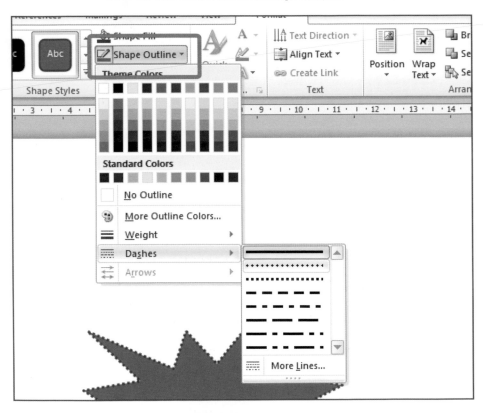

3 From the drop-down menu, choose an outline colour, weight (thickness) and line style.

When adding a shape to your document, you can create a perfect square or circle – or constrain the proportions of other shapes – by holding down the **Shift** key while you drag.

Add shadow effects

1 Select the shape.

2 On the **Format** tab, click **Shape Effects**.

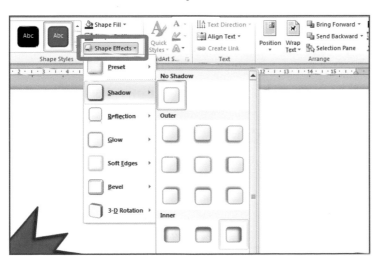

3 From the drop-down menu, move your cursor over 'Shadow' to see a list of shadow presets. Move your cursor over the options to see a live preview of the effect in your document.

4 Click a shadow effect to apply it to your shape.

Rotate a shape in 3D

1 Select the shape.

2 On the **Format** tab, in the 'Shape Styles' group, click **Shape Effects**.

3 Move your cursor over '3-D Rotation'. A drop-down menu will appear.

4 Choose a rotation preset. For more precise control, click **3-D Rotation Options...** to type in custom values.

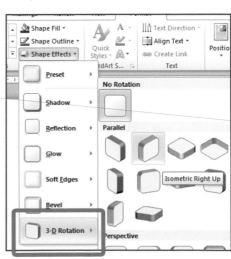

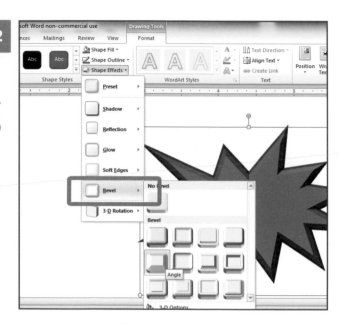

Apply a bevel effect

1 Select the shape.

2 On the **Format** tab, click **Shape Effects** from the 'Shape Styles' group.

3 Hover the cursor over a shape you are looking for, in this case 'Bevel'.

4 From the drop-down menu, click a preset, in this case **Angle**.

5 Click **3-D Options** at the bottom of this menu if you prefer to use custom values. In the 'Format Shape' dialog box that appears, you can also choose a shape's material to order to give it a plastic or metal look, as well as change the lighting type to determine how a shape is illuminated.

Change a shape into another shape

1 Click the shape that you want to change to a different shape.

2 On the **Format** tab, in the 'Insert Shapes' group, click **Edit Shape**.

3 Move your cursor over the 'Change Shape' field, and click the new shape that you want, in this case **Right Arrow Callout**.

Do more with shapes

Once you've mastered the basics of selecting shapes to use in your Word document, you can look at creating your own.

Draw a freeform shape

Even though Word offers lots of shapes to choose from, you may want to create your own freeform shape. You can also create a shape that looks like it was hand drawn.

1 On the **Insert** tab, in the 'Illustrations' group, click **Shapes**.

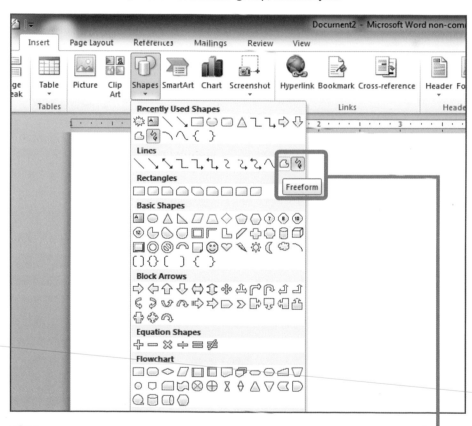

2 Under 'Lines', move your cursor over the options to indentify them and then click either:

■ **Freeform:** to draw a shape with both curved and straight segments.

■ **Scribble:** to draw a shape that looks as if it was drawn with a pen by hand, or to create smooth curves.

3 Click in your document, and then drag to draw. To draw a straight segment, click one location, move the cursor to another place, and then click again.

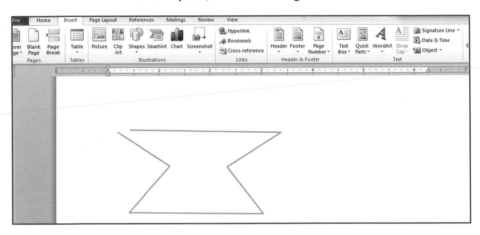

4 When you've finished drawing, either double click to leave the shape open or to close the shape, click near its starting point.

Edit the points of your shape

You can easily tweak a shape supplied by Microsoft or a freeform by editing its points.

1 Select the shape that you want to edit.

2 On the **Format** tab, in the 'Insert Shapes' group, click **Edit Shape**, and then click **Edit Points**.

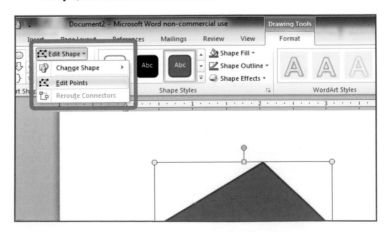

3 Drag one of the vertexes that outline the shape.

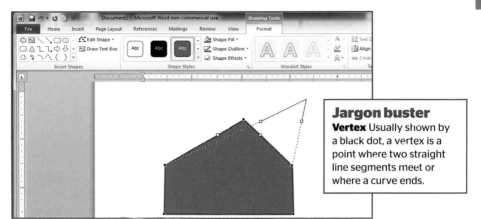

Jargon buster
Vertex Usually shown by a black dot, a vertex is a point where two straight line segments meet or where a curve ends.

Add text to a shape

1 Right click the shape you wish to add text to.

2 From the pop-up menu, choose **Add Text**.

3 Type your text into the shape.

4 To quickly format the text, select it and right click to access the quick formatting panel.

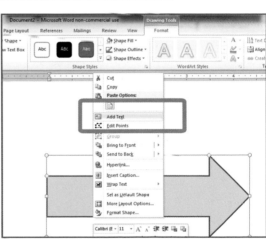

5 To edit the text, first right click the shape and select **Edit Text**.

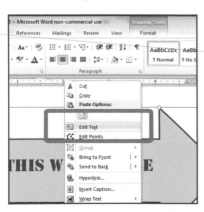

Photos and graphics

Add a gradient fill to a shape

To apply a gradient fill to your shape, you can choose one from Word's built-in gradient fills or create your own customised gradient fill.

1 Select the shape that you wish to apply a gradient fill to.

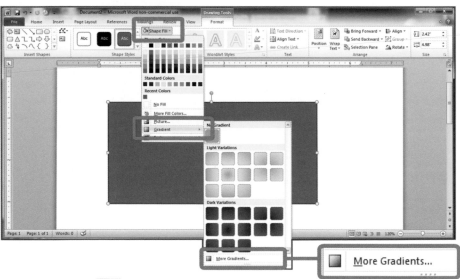

More Gradients...

2 On the **Format** tab, in the 'Shape Styles' group, click **Shape Fill**.

3 From the drop-down menu, select a fill colour from 'Theme Colors' or 'Standard Colors'.

4 Then move your cursor over 'Gradient', and select a gradient from the 'Light' and 'Dark' variations shown on the drop-down menu.

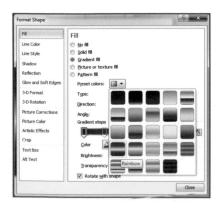

5 Alternatively, to apply a built-in gradient to your shape, select **More Gradients...** from the bottom of the drop-down menu.

6 In the 'Format Shape' dialog box select **Gradient fill**. In the 'Preset colors' list, select a gradient (in this case **Rainbow**).

Gradient fills can be applied to text boxes and SmartArt graphics too (see pages 118–19 and 129).

Create a custom gradient fill

1 Follow Steps 1-6 opposite to reach the 'Format Shape' dialog box.

2 In the 'Type' list, select the type of gradient that you want, such as **Linear**.

3 In the 'Direction' list, select the direction the gradient will take, in this case **Diagonal: top left to bottom right**.

4 Under 'Gradient stops', click **Add gradient stops** or **Remove gradient stops** until you have a stop for each of the colours in your gradient fill. A 'stop' is the point where the blending of two adjacent colours in a gradient ends. You can have between 2 and 10 stops.

5 You can continue to customise the gradient fill by selecting the following for each of the colours used. First click one of the stops and then:

In the 'Color' list: select the colour that you want.

In the 'Position' box: type the position that you want.

You can also adjust the **Brightness** or **Transparency** of the colour.

6 When you have finished, click **Close**.

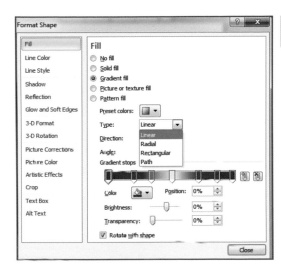

Jargon buster

Gradient fill This is a fill that gradually changes from one colour to another. In Word you can choose from the following fills: Linear, Radial, Rectangular and Path. Linear changes colours in a straight line; Radial radiates colours in a circle; Rectangular radiates colours outwards in a box shape and Path radiates colours inwards from the outline/path of the shape.

Create a text box

Text boxes are a great way to draw your reader's attention to a particular piece of text or link information to images such as with a caption. Using text boxes means, for example, you can easily move text around your document and, as with shapes, you can apply similar effects to text boxes.

Add a text box

1 On the **Insert** tab, in the 'Text' group, click **Text Box**.

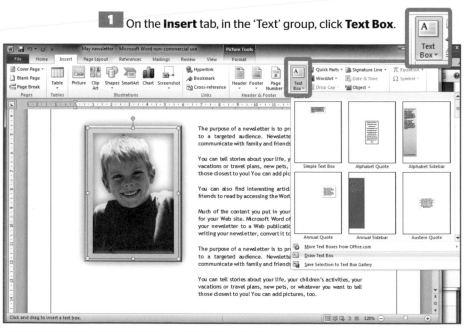

2 From the drop-down menu click **Draw Text Box**.

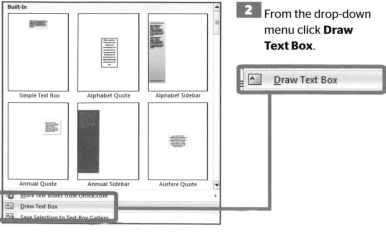

3 Click and drag on the page to create the text box. In this instance, as a caption box beneath the photograph.

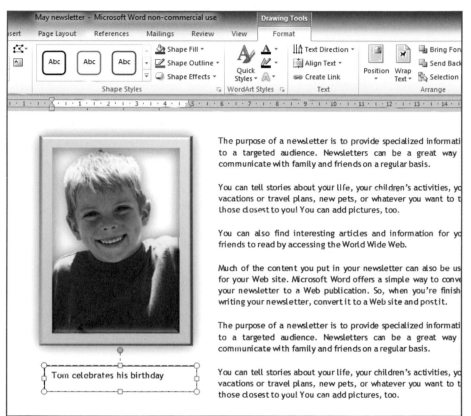

4 Type your text inside the text box.

Alternatively at step 2, select one of the built-in text boxes from the drop-down menu. These have a pre-defined size and position as well as colours and fonts. Once you select a built-in text box, it will appear automatically on the page.

Make changes to a text box

You can make changes to your text box – everything from size, position, border style, fill colour to 3D effects and rotation can be altered to suit. Simply treat your text box as a shape and follow the steps on pages 106–12 to make adjustments.

Style text with WordArt

Add effects to the text inside a text box using WordArt – Word's text styling feature. You can change fill and line colour, add shadows or bevels or create special text effects such as curved, slanted or 3D text.

Add WordArt

1 On the **Insert** tab, in the 'Text' group, click **WordArt** and then click the WordArt style that you want.

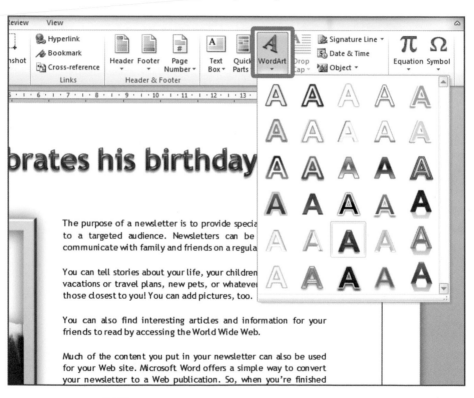

2 Type in your text.

Add or modify text effects

1 Select the text box, or some text inside the text box.

2 On the **Format** tab in the 'WordArt Styles' group, click **Text Effects**. A drop-down menu appears showing the different effect categories.

3 Move your cursor over one of the effect categories to see a second drop-down menu of preset effects.

4 Hover your cursor over a preset to see a live preview.

5 Select an effect preset. The effect will be applied to your text. You can combine several different WordArt effects on one piece of text.

Tip
You can convert existing text to WordArt. Select the text and on the **Insert** tab, in the 'Text' group, click **WordArt**, and then click the WordArt style that you want. Word will create a text box for your text and apply the style to the text.

Rotate WordArt

As with pictures, shapes and text boxes, you can rotate your WordArt using the rotation handle (the green circle on the image). Simply drag the handle in the direction you wish to rotate the WordArt. Alternatively, you can use the 'Format Shape' dialog box to set a precise degree of rotation.

1 Click the WordArt to select it.

2 On the **Format** tab, in the 'Arrange' group, click **Rotate**, and then **More Rotation Options**....

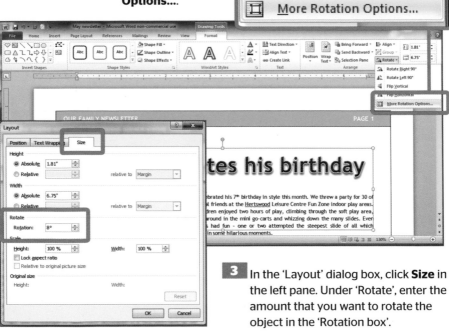

3 In the 'Layout' dialog box, click **Size** in the left pane. Under 'Rotate', enter the amount that you want to rotate the object in the 'Rotation box'.

Flip WordArt

1 Click the WordArt to select it.

2 On the **Format** tab, in the 'Arrange' group, click **Rotate**.

3 From the drop-down menu, either click **Flip Vertical** to reverse the WordArt vertically or click **Flip Horizontal** to reverse it horizontally.

Tip

To quickly rotate your WordArt by 90 degrees, click the WordArt to select it and then on the **Format** tab, in the 'Arrange' group, click **Rotate**. Either click **Rotate Right 90°** to rotate it to the right, or to rotate the object 90 degrees to the left, click **Rotate Left 90°**.

Arrange shapes and objects

Your Word document may contain several elements such as shapes, WordArt and text boxes but it can be fiddly and time-consuming positioning items individually. Fortunately, Word has several tools that can help arrange objects on the page. You can select and then arrange several items at once.

Align two or more objects

1 Select the objects to align by holding down the **Ctrl** key and clicking on each in turn.

2 On the **Format** tab, in the 'Arrange' group, click **Align**.

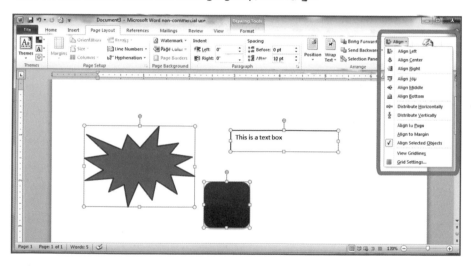

3 From the drop-down menu, select one of the six alignment options at the top of the menu.

4 The objects will align to each other based on the option that you choose to select.

Distribute objects evenly

To make a document with several objects in a row or to make a column look neater, you can position them at an equal distance from one another. This can be done either horizontally or vertically.

1 Select the objects to align by holding down the **Ctrl** key and clicking on each in turn.

Photos and graphics

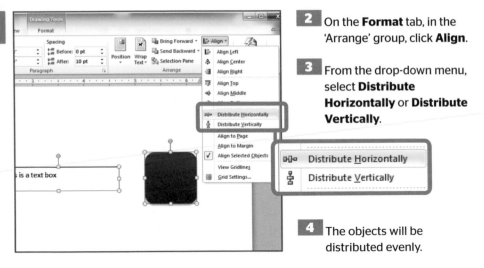

2 On the **Format** tab, in the 'Arrange' group, click **Align**.

3 From the drop-down menu, select **Distribute Horizontally** or **Distribute Vertically**.

4 The objects will be distributed evenly.

Stack objects

You can stack items so that one appears in front of another or even change the order in which each appears on the document.

1 Select the object you wish to move.

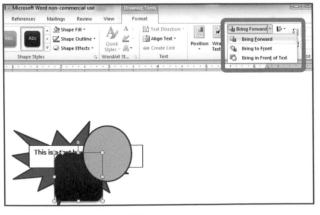

2 On the **Format** tab, in the 'Arrange' group, do one of the following:

    To move it one step closer to the front of the stack, click **Bring Forward**.

    To move it to the top of the stack, click the arrow next to 'Bring Forward', and then click **Bring to Front**.

To move it in front of text, click the arrow next to 'Bring Forward', and then click **Bring in Front of Text**.

To move it one step down in the stack, click **Send Backward**.

To move it to the bottom of the stack, click the arrow next to 'Send Backward', and then click **Send to Back**.

To move it behind text, click the arrow next to 'Send Backward', and then click **Send Behind Text**.

Group objects

Rather than selecting multiple objects each time you want to move
or change them, Word lets you group shapes, text boxes and other
elements into one object. You can then rotate, flip, move and resize
the objects at the same time as if they were a single item. You can
also change the format of all the items within a group at once – for
example by adding a fill colour or shape effects.

Group objects

1 Select the objects you wish to group by holding down the **Ctrl**
key and clicking on each in turn.

2 On the **Format** tab, in the 'Arrange' group, click the
Group button, and then click **Group**.

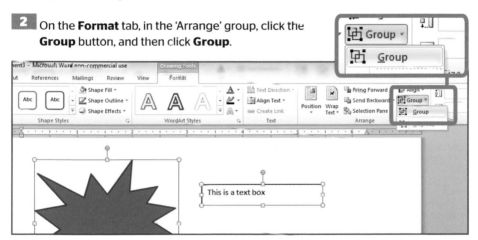

3 The objects will now be
grouped. There will be
a single box with sizing
handles around the
entire group to show
they are one object.

Even after you have grouped several
objects, you can still select a single
object within the group. Select the
group, and then click the individual
object that you want to select.

Ungroup objects

1 Select the group that you want to ungroup.

2 On the **Format** tab, in the 'Arrange group', click **Group**, and
then click **Ungroup**. The items will appear ungrouped.

Add SmartArt graphics

A feature of Microsoft Office, SmartArt graphics are predrawn diagrams and illustrations that can be inserted into your Office documents. You can edit the diagrams and change the style without having to fiddle with shape size and alignment, as SmartArt graphics automatically adjust to maintain their overall shape and design.

Create a SmartArt graphic

1 Click on the page where you want the SmartArt graphic to be placed. On the **Insert** tab, in the 'Illustration' group, click **SmartArt**.

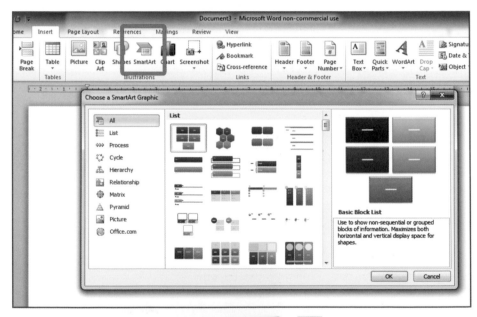

SmartArt graphics work best when the number of shapes in the layout and the text they contain are limited to just key points. The 'Trapezoid List' is the best choice for larger amounts of text.

2 Select a category in the left pane of the dialog box.

3 In the centre pane, click on one of the layouts in this category to see a more detailed view in the right pane of the dialog box.

4 Click a SmartArt graphic and click **OK**.

Add text to a SmartArt graphic

1 Select the graphic. Click the arrow on the left side of the graphic.

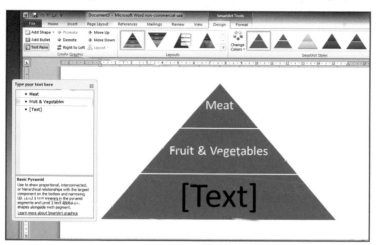

2 Enter text next to each bullet in the task pane. It appears in the graphic, resizing automatically to fit inside the shape.

Add or delete a shape

1 Select the SmartArt graphic.

2 From the **Design** tab, click **Add Shape** in the 'Graphics' group.

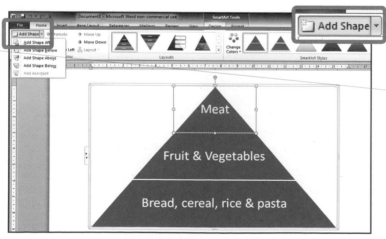

Tip
To quickly move shapes in a SmartArt graphic up (promote) and down (demote), use the task pane. Place the cursor in the task pane, press **Tab** to demote a shape. Press the **Backspace** key (or **Shift+Tab**) to promote a shape.

3 Click the shape that's positioned closest to where you want to add the new shape.

4 Select **Add Shape Before** or **Add Shape After**.

5 If you want to add a superior or a subordinate shape, select either the **Add Shape Above** or **Add Shape Below** options.

6 To delete a shape, click the shape, and then press the **Delete** key on your keyboard. To delete the entire SmartArt graphic, click the border of the SmartArt graphic, and then press **Delete**.

Change the SmartArt style

1 Select the graphic.

2 On the **Design** tab in the 'SmartArt Styles' group, click the 'More' **drop-down arrow** to view all of the styles.

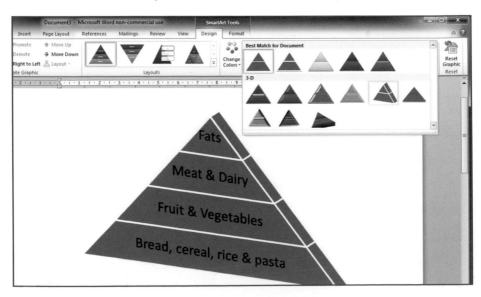

3 Move your cursor over a style to see a live preview.

4 Click a style to apply it.

Change the colour of a SmartArt graphic

Word offers a range of colour schemes to use with its SmartArt graphics.

Tip
To add a new shape, place your cursor in the bullet list where you want the new shape to appear and press **Enter**. A new bullet will appear in the task pane, and a new shape will appear in the graphic.

1 Click the SmartArt graphic.

2 On the **Design** tab, click **Change Colors**.

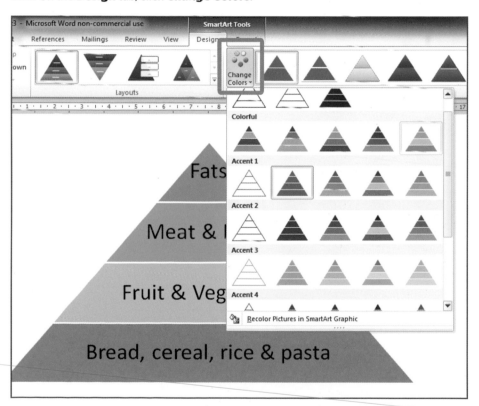

3 From the drop-down menu, choose a colour scheme.

To change the look of just one shape in a SmartArt graphic, select the shape and click the Format tab. You can then change the Shape Style, colour, effects and other settings.

Get started with tables

There are a couple of ways to add a table to your Word document. You can later modify the table by adding, removing or resizing rows and columns.

Use a table template

You can choose from a gallery of pre-formatted table templates. These come with sample data so you can see how your table will look when you add your own data.

1 Click on the page where you want to insert a table.

2 On the **Insert** tab, in the 'Tables' group, click **Table**.

3 Click **Quick Tables**, and then click the template that you want.

4 Replace the data in the template with your own information.

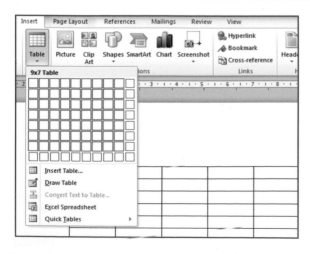

Use the Table menu

1 Click on the page where you want to insert a table.

2 On the **Insert** tab, in the 'Tables' group, click **Table**.

3 Drag your cursor over the diagram squares to select the number of rows and columns that you want.

Use the Insert Table command

Using this command you can choose the table dimensions and format before you insert the table into a document.

1 Click where you want to insert a table.

2 On the **Insert** tab, in the 'Tables' group, click **Table**, and then click **Insert Table…**.

3 Enter the number of columns and rows in the 'Table size' field.

4 Under 'AutoFit behavior', choose options to adjust the table size.

Convert text to a table

1 Select the text you wish to convert to a table.

2 On the **Insert** tab, click **Table**.

3 Select **Convert Text to Table…** from the drop-down menu.

4 In the dialog box, under 'Separate text at', choose one of the options to tell Word how to divide the text into each column.

5 Click **OK** and the text appears in a table.

Get started with tables

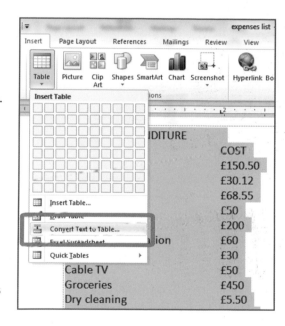

Insert Table

Table size

Number of columns: 5

Number of rows: 2

AutoFit behavior

◉ Fixed column width: Auto

○ AutoFit to contents

○ AutoFit to window

☐ Remember dimensions for new tables

OK   Cancel

Add a row or a column

1 Right click in a cell above or below where you want to add a row or to the left or to the right of where you want to add a column.

2 On the pop-up menu, click **Insert**, and then **Insert Columns to the Left**, **Insert Columns to the Right**, **Insert Rows Above** or **Insert Rows Below**.

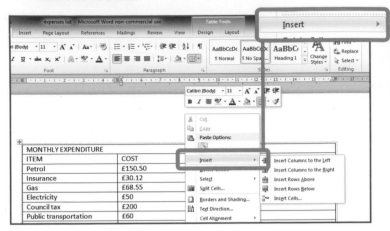

Delete a row or column

1 Select the row or column.

2 Right click your mouse.

3 From the pop-up menu click **Delete cells**.

4 In the 'Delete Cells' dialog box, select **Delete entire row** or **Delete entire column**. Click **OK**.

Change column width and row height by dragging

1 Hover your cursor over the right border of the column or on the bottom border of the row you want to change. The cursor will change into a resize pointer.

2 Drag the border to increase or decrease the size.

Change a column width precisely

1 Right click the table you wish to adjust and from the pop-up menu, click **Table Properties...**.

2 In the 'Table Properties' dialog box click the **Column** tab.

3 Click **Previous Column** or **Next Column** to select the column you want to adjust. (If necessary, you can drag the dialog box to one side to see the table beneath it).

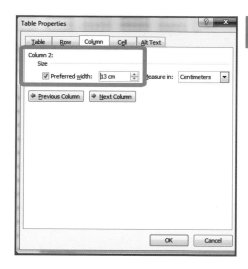

4 Click the **Preferred Width** check box, and set a width in centimetres or as a percentage of the width of the table.

5 Click **OK**.

Change a row height precisely

1 Right click the table you wish to adjust and from the pop-up menu, click **Table Properties...**.

2 In the 'Table Properties' dialog box click the **Row** tab.

3 Click **Previous Row** or **Next Row** to select the row you want to adjust.

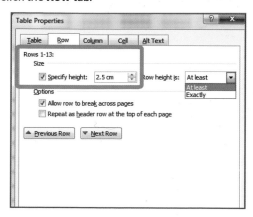

4 Click the **Specify height** check box, and set a width in centimetres or as a percentage of the table width. You can set the row height to be at least or exactly this measurement.

5 Click **OK**.

Change the look of a table

Word provides lots of control over how your table looks. You can make changes to text and table formatting, add borders, make colour fills and adjust individual settings for cells, columns and row. But if you're in a hurry, Word can help with a pre-defined style for your table.

Apply a table style

1 Click anywhere on the table.

2 On the **Design** tab, click the 'More' **drop-down arrow** in 'Table Styles'.

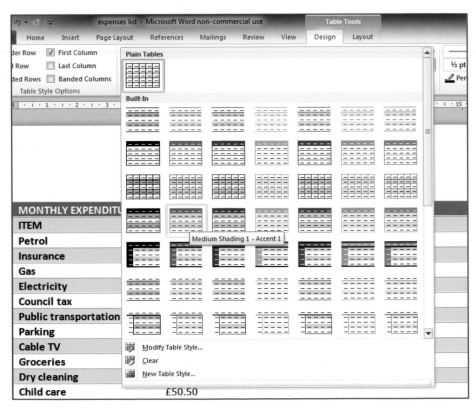

3 This will show all the available table styles. Move your cursor over a style to see a live preview.

4 Click on a style to apply it your table.

Add borders to a table

1 Select the cells that you wish to add a border to. If you want to add a border to the table select all the cells.

2 On the **Design** tab, choose a **Line Style**, **Line Weight** (thickness) and **Pen Color**.

3 Click the 'Borders' **drop-down arrow**.

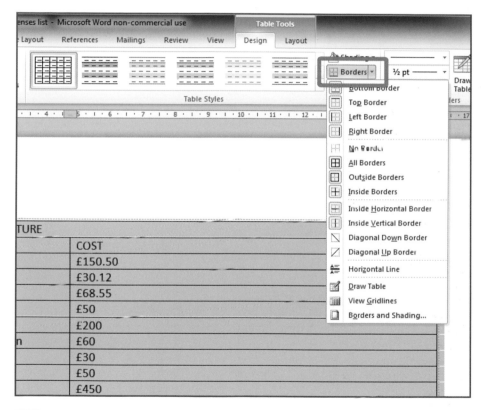

4 From the drop-down menu, select the desired border type.

5 The border will be added to the cells you have selected.

Further table modifications

When you select a table in Word, two tabs appear under 'Table Tools' on the Ribbon – the 'Design' and the 'Layout' tabs. Using commands on the 'Layout' tab, you can make a variety of changes to the table. Here are some of the text adjustments you can make.

Align text in cells

Just as with paragraphs, text in a cell can be aligned left, centre or right. It can also be aligned vertically: top, middle or bottom.

1 Select the cell whose text alignment you wish to change.

2 On the **Layout** tab, click one of the buttons in the 'Alignment' group to apply.

Fit text in cells

Microsoft Word usually wraps text in a table cell automatically. However, if your rows are set to an exact height, the cells won't expand as you add text to them. To overcome this, you can set the row height to change to allow for all the text that you add. Here's how:

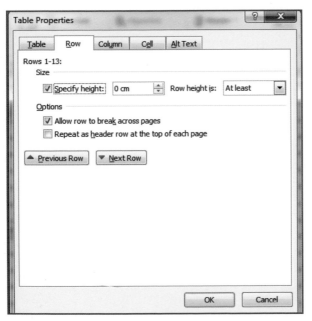

1 Move your cursor over the table. A small square will appear at the top left of the table. Click this to select the table.

2 Right click the table, click **Table Properties...**, and then click the **Row** tab.

3 Tick the **Specify height** box.

4 Click the 'Row height is' **drop-down arrow**, and then click **At least**. Click **OK**.

5 To show all the text, right click the selected table and then click **Distribute Rows Evenly**.

Change text direction

Normally, text is oriented from left to right but you can use the 'Text Direction' button to change the way text reads in a cell or group of selected cells.

1 Select the text in the table that you wish to adjust.

2 On the **Layout** tab, in the 'Alignment' group, click **Text Direction**.

3 By clicking **Text Direction** once, the text direction changes to top-to-bottom. Click it again and the direction is changed to bottom-to-top. Clicking it a third time restores the text to its original direction.

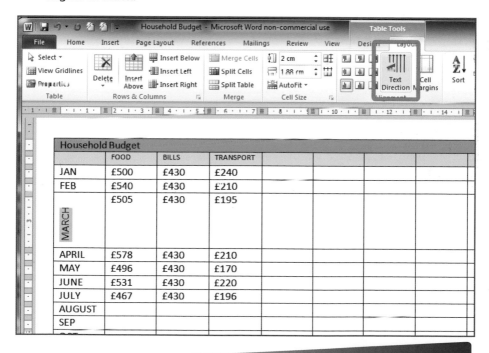

Once you've changed the text direction for a cell, you'll see that the alignment, lists and indents options on the Home, Page Layout and Table Tool Layout tabs change orientation to match.

Merge cells

You can merge cells by combining two or more cells into one large cell. Merged cells are useful when you want to create a header that spans the width of a table, or use large graphics in your table.

1 Select the cells you want to combine (in this case, the Household Budget row).

2 On the **Layout** tab, in the 'Merge' group, click **Merge Cells**. Alternatively, right click the cells and from the pop-up menu click **Merge Cells**.

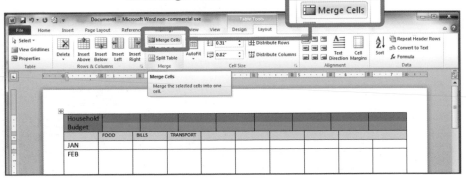

3 Any content will now span the large merged cell.

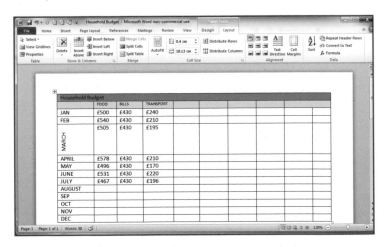

Split cells

You can achieve the opposite effect of merging by splitting a cell into multiple columns and/or rows.

1 Select the cell or cells that you want to split into more columns or rows (in this case, the Household Budget row once again).

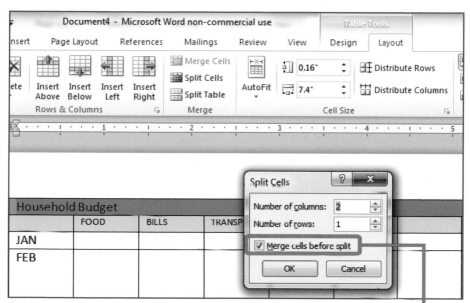

2 On the **Layout** tab, in the 'Merge' group, click **Split Cells**.

3 In the 'Split Cells' dialog box do one or both of the following:
- Enter a value in the 'Number of columns' field to divide the selected cell vertically.
- Enter a value in the 'Number of rows' field to divide the selected cells horizontally.

4 The 'Merge Cells Before Split' check box is ticked by default. This means that Word treats the merged cell as one and splits it into the number of rows or columns you've entered. To split each selected cell into the number of rows or columns entered, click on the **Merge Cells Before Split** check box to clear it.

5 Click **OK**.

Change cell margins

You can change the distance between content and the cell borders either for the entire table or for selected cells.

1 To set margins for all the cells in a table, select the entire table and then right click. From the pop-up menu click **Table Properties...**.

2 On the **Table** tab, click **Options**.

3 In the 'Table Options' dialog box, under 'Default cell margins', enter new values in the 'Top', 'Bottom', 'Left' and 'Right' fields.

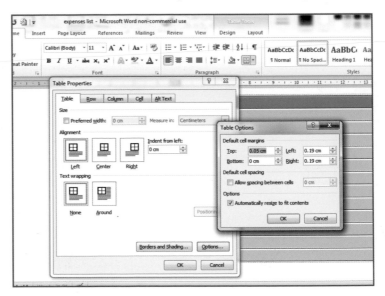

4 Click **OK** twice.

5 To set margins for all selected cells, select the cells you wish to change, and then follow Steps 1 and 2. In the 'Cell Options' dialog box, click on the **Same as the whole table** check box to untick it. Then enter new values in the 'Top', 'Bottom', 'Left' and 'Right' values.

6 Click **OK** twice.

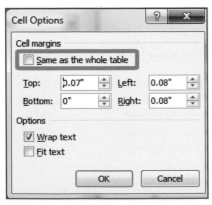

Do more with Word

By reading and following all the steps in this chapter, you will get to grips with:

- Using Mail Merge
- Making and tracking comments
- Sharing your documents safely

Use Mail Merge

Word's Mail Merge is a handy feature that lets you create a single document for multiple recipients using information that is stored in a list or spreadsheet. It's a great timesaver when creating letters, name tags and labels that contain the same basic information but also require personal details, such as name and address, of the respective recipient.

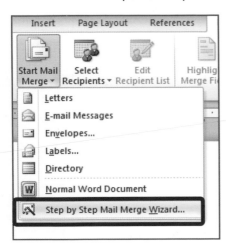

Open the Mail Merge Wizard

1 Open an existing Word document, or create a new one.

2 On the **Mailings** tab, click **Start Mail Merge**.

3 Click **Step by Step Mail Merge Wizard...**.

4 This opens the Mail Merge Wizard, which guides you through the steps required to complete a mail merge.

Create a Mail Merge

In this example we've used a letter that, when printed, will consist of the same basic message, but have different personal information (such as the name and address) for each recipient.

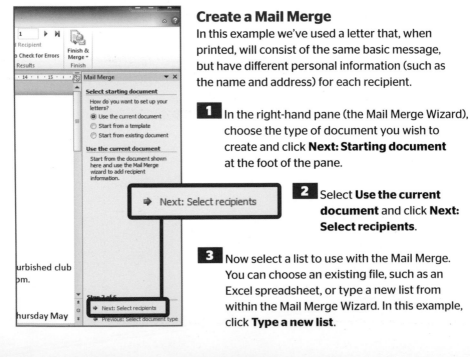

1 In the right-hand pane (the Mail Merge Wizard), choose the type of document you wish to create and click **Next: Starting document** at the foot of the pane.

2 Select **Use the current document** and click **Next: Select recipients**.

3 Now select a list to use with the Mail Merge. You can choose an existing file, such as an Excel spreadsheet, or type a new list from within the Mail Merge Wizard. In this example, click **Type a new list**.

4 Enter the recipient information that you want to use.

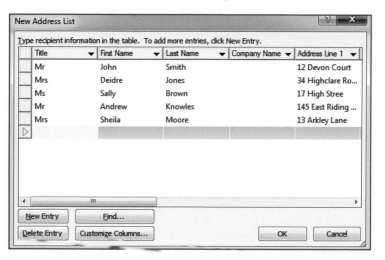

5 When finished click **OK**. A 'Save As' dialog box will pop up, allowing you to save the recipient list.

6 In the 'Mail Merge Recipients' dialog box, you can tick or untick those recipients to be used in the mail merge. Click **OK** and then **Next: Write your letter** at the foot of the 'Mail Merge' dialog box.

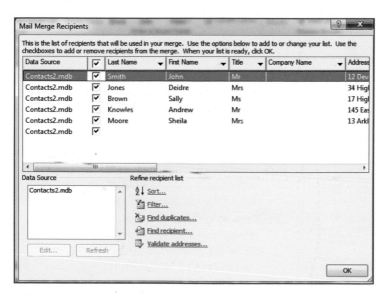

Add recipient information

Now in your letter, you need to add placeholders for the recipient data, so that mail merge knows exactly where to add the data.

1 In the document click where you wish the information to appear. Select 'Address block', Greeting line', 'Electronic postage' or 'More items' from the task pane.

2 Depending on what you've chosen, a dialog box may appear. Select the options you want and click **OK**.

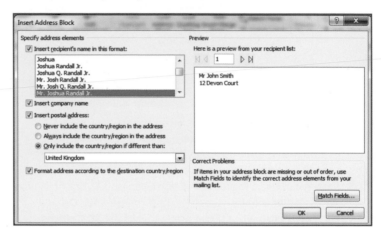

3 A placeholder appears in your document. For example: «AddressBlock».

4 Repeat these steps for each piece of recipient data in the letter. Then click **Next: Preview your letters**.

BE CAREFUL!

Take care when creating a mail merge to avoid introducing errors in the individual documents. Proof your base document carefully before completing the merge process. For example, make sure you have included enough fields for all the recipient addresses and that spacing exists between all the fields.

5 Preview the letter to ensure the information from the recipient list appears correctly. Click **Next: Complete the merge**.

6 Click **Print**. In the 'Merge to Printer' dialog box, click **All**, and then click **OK**. In the 'Print' dialog box, adjust the print settings if needed, and then click **OK**.

Review documents

Having created what you believe is the perfect document in Word, you may want to let others review it for you. Whether this is a colleague at work, a friend or family member, a second pair of eyes can make a huge difference when it comes to spotting mistakes, inconsistencies and other errors.

On a printed copy of your document, your reviewers can use a coloured pen to mark errors, cross out sentence or add comments, but Word lets you do all these things on the electronic version using its Track Changes and Comments features. Furthermore, you can see all the changes that have been suggested by others before deciding whether to make those changes permanent.

Turn on Track Changes

When you select Word's **Track Changes** option, every change made to your document will show as a coloured markup. For example, if you add text, it will be underlined. If you delete text, it won't disappear from the page as normal, but instead will have a strike (line) through it.

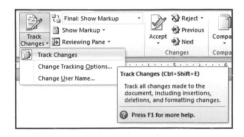

1 Click the **Review** tab.

2 Click the **Track Changes** command.

3 Now if you make a change to the document, it will show as a coloured markup. The colour of the markups will vary by reviewer. This way, if several people review your document you can tell at a glance which person has made each change.

4 Click **Track Changes** again to turn it off.

Tip

You can view and change the way Word marks tracked changes by clicking the **Review** tab and then **Track Changes**. From the drop-down menu click **Change Tracking Options...**. Here in the 'Track Changes Options' box you can change the formatting of how insertions, deletions and moved text look.

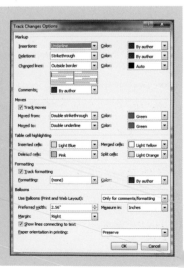

Add a comment

Sometimes, rather than adding or deleting text, you may want to make a note about the content. You can do this by adding a comment, which appears in a balloon shaped box in the right margin.

1 Select the text or place your cursor next to where you want the comment to appear.

2 On the **Review** tab, click **New Comment**.

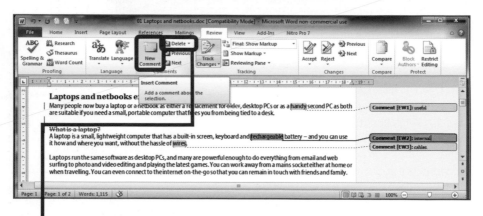

3 Type your comment.

Delete comments

1 Select the balloon with the comment you wish to delete.

2 On the **Review** tab, click **Delete**.

3 To delete all the comments in a document, click the 'Delete' **drop-down arrow** on the **Review** tab. From the drop-down menu, click **Delete All Comments in Document**.

Accept or reject changes

Tracked changes and comments are merely suggestions. To become permanent, you need to accept them. Or if you disagree with the suggested change you can reject them.

1 Select the change you want to accept or reject.

2 On the **Review** tab, click either **Accept** or **Reject**.

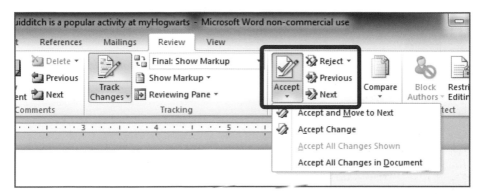

3 If you then click on **Accept Change**, the markup will disappear, and the text appears as normal.

Accepting or rejecting all the changes in your document doesn't affect comments. You must delete these separately.

Accept all changes

1 On the **Review** tab, click the 'Accept' **drop-down arrow**.

2 From the drop-down menu click **Accept All Changes in Document**.

Reject all changes

1 On the **Review** tab, click the 'Reject' **drop-down arrow**.

2 From the drop-down menu click **Reject All Changes in Document**.

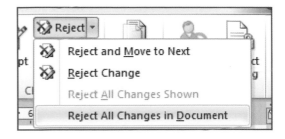

Hide tracked changes

If your document has lots of tracked changes, it may be confusing trying to read it but Word lets you hide markups or change how they appear.

1 On the **Review** tab, in the 'Tracking' group, click the 'Final: Show Markup' **drop-down arrow**.

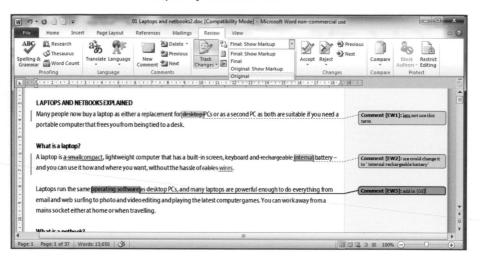

2 From the drop-down menu, choose one of the four options:

■ **Final: Show Markup:** this is the default view for all documents opened in Word. It shows the final document with all tracked changes and comments.

■ **Final:** shows the final version and hides all markups. However, tracked changes or comments that haven't been accepted, rejected or deleted remain in the document.

■ **Original: Show Markup:** shows the original version along with tracked changes and comments.

■ **Original:** shows the original document and hides tracked changes and comments. Tracked changes or comments that haven't been accepted, rejected or deleted remain in the document.

3 Choose **Final** or **Original** from the drop-down menu to hide the markups.

Use the Document Inspector

Before you share the final version of your document with others, you can use Word's Document Inspector to find and remove content that you don't want other people to see – useful if you have comments or tracked changes in your document. It's best to first create, and then inspect, a copy of your original document, as you may not be able to restore information that the Document Inspector removes.

1 Open the document you wish to inspect.

2 Click the **File** tab, and then click **Info** from the left sidebar.

3 Under the 'Prepare for Sharing' option, click **Check for Issues** and from the drop-down menu, choose **Inspect Document**.

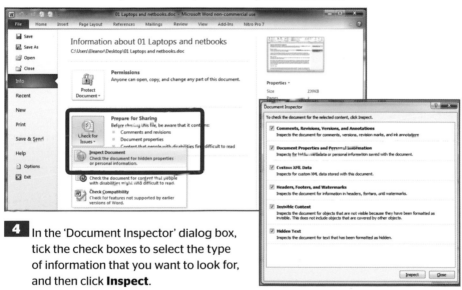

4 In the 'Document Inspector' dialog box, tick the check boxes to select the type of information that you want to look for, and then click **Inspect**.

5 The inspection results are shown in the 'Document Inspector' dialog box, listed beneath each category heading. Categories that have potential sensitive data have an exclamation mark next to them.

6 Click **Remove All** next to those categories from which you wish to remove hidden information.

7 Click **Close**.

Protect a document

If you're ready to share your document with others but want to stop them from making changes to it, use Word's protection options to safeguard your document. There are several layers of protection available from simple read-only restrictions to applying a digital signature.

1 With your document open, click the **File** tab.

2 In the Backstage view, click **Info**.

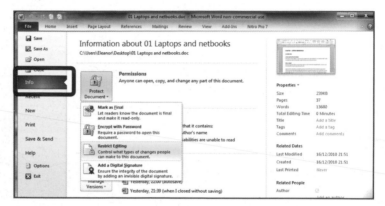

3 In 'Permissions', click **Protect Document**. Choose from the following options:

■ **Mark as Final:** makes the document read-only. No changes or additions can then be made to the document.

■ **Encrypt with Password:** lets you set a password so that only those who know the password can open the document.

■ **Restrict Editing:** lets you determine what types of changes can be made to the document including formatting and editing restrictions.

■ **Add a Digital Signature:** this adds a visible or invisible digital signature.

Jargon buster
Digital signature An electronic and encrypted stamp of authentication used on digital information such as documents or email messages. A digital signature confirms that the information originated from the signer and has not been altered.

Tip
If you have a Microsoft Live ID, you'll see a further option in Step 3 called 'Restrict Permission by People'. This uses Microsoft's IRM (Information Right Management) Service to restrict or assign permission to certain users.

Resources

Keyboard shortcuts

Press these keys	To do this
Ctrl + N	Create a new document
Ctrl + O	Open a document
Ctrl + W	Close a document
Ctrl + S	Save a document
Esc	Cancel an action
Ctrl + Home	Move to the beginning of a document
Ctrl + End	Move to the end of a document
Backspace	Delete one character to the left
Ctrl + Backspace	Delete one word to the left
Delete	Delete one character to the right
Ctrl + Delete	Delete one word to the right
Ctrl + A	Select all the text in a document
Ctrl + C	Copy the selected text or object
Ctrl + X	Cut the selected text or object
Ctrl + V	Paste text or an object
Ctrl + Alt + V	Open the 'Paste Special' dialog box, which allows you choose how text or images are added to the document
Ctrl + D	Launch the 'Font' dialog box
Ctrl + F	Find text
Ctrl + Z	Undo an action
Ctrl + Y	Redo or repeat an action
Ctrl + Shift + spacebar	Insert a non-breaking space
Ctrl + Shift + Enter	Create a column break
Ctrl + Shift + L	Apply bullets
Ctrl + Shift + A	Convert selected text to capital letters or vice versa
Ctrl + Shift + F	Display the 'Font' dialog box
Ctrl + Shift + P	Font size select
Ctrl +]	Increase font size one point
Ctrl + B	Bold text
Ctrl + I	Italicise text
Ctrl + U	Underline text
Ctrl + Spacebar	Remove a paragraph or character formatting
Ctrl + J	Justify a paragraph
Ctrl + L	Left align a paragraph
Ctrl + E	Centre a paragraph
Ctrl + R	Right align a paragraph

Jargon buster

AutoCorrect A Word feature that automatically corrects spelling or replaces text with pre-determined entries.

Bitmap A bitmap is a file format used to store a digital image. To bitmap something means to turn it into an bitmap image.

Cell In tables, a cell is a box at the intersection of a row and a column, into which you enter a single piece of information or data.

Clip art Ready-made artwork that's included with Word or downloaded from the web for use in your documents.

Centered text Text placed at an equal distance from the left and right margins.

Compression Digital files can be compressed using mathematical algorithms to create smaller files that take up less storage space and are easier to share. Digital photos, video, music files are commonly compressed.

Crop A photo-editing term that means removing unwanted areas from a photo.

Cursor A cursor is the symbol on the screen that shows you where the next character will appear.

Cut To remove selected text, file or image from its position to the clipboard.

Dialog box A window that pops up to display or request information.

Digital signature See page 150.

Drag and drop To move an item on screen by clicking it, holding the left mouse button down while moving the mouse, then releasing the button where you want it to be positioned.

Drop-down menu A list of options that appears when you click a menu name or button, usually marked with a down-pointing arrow.

Embedded file Describes a file that is stored within another file.

Field An area or container on screen that holds information.

File format See page 23.

Font A set of letters and numbers in a particular style.

Font size The size at which a font appears on screen or printed. Measured in points, or pt for short.

Footer A special area at the bottom of a Word page. You can add text to have it appear on every page of the document.

Format To apply attributes such as typeface, font size, and colour to text or elements of a document.

Gradient fill See page 117.

Gutter The area between adjacent columns in a document.

Header An area at the top of the page that can be used for information about the document and/or the author of the document. Similar to a Footer.

Hyperlink See page 78.

Icon A small picture that represents an object or program.

Indent The area between a page's margin and where the text begins. Normally, the first line of a paragraph is indented, and the remaining lines in the paragraph are flush against the margin of the page.

Justify To align horizontally so that text and other objects are spread evenly across a page. Justified text has the same left and right margins.

Margin The area between the edge of a page and where text and/or objects can be placed in a document.

Orphan A single line of a paragraph at the top of a page or column.

Page break A command that divides page content and forces content after the break to start on a new page.

Placeholder text Also known as dummy text. A piece of text – sometime nonsense text such as lorem ipsum – designed to show the position, font, size and format of text in a layout.

Point Refers to the size of type – a point is the smallest unit of measure.

Pop-up A small window that appears next to an item on screen to give additional information.

Saturation How rich the colours are in a digital image.

Sharpness The clarity of detail in a photo.

Sizing handles See page 92.

Status bar A horizontal line of information shown at the bottom or top of a program window.

Tab stops Preset points in a column or text box, where the cursor will stop when the Tab key is pressed.

Taskbar A bar that runs across the bottom of your screen, from where you can open programs and access key Windows functions.

Text alignment Describes the position of text within margins.

Title bar The part of a computer window – usually at the top – where the name of the window is shown.

Track changes A Word feature that lets you view changes that have been made to a document. Useful when several people make revisions of the document.

Vertex Usually shown by a black dot, a vertex is a point where two straight line segments meet or where a curve ends.

Widow A single line of a paragraph that is left at the bottom of a page or column.

Wizard An interactive help file that guides you through a step-by-step process to choose settings or accomplish a task.

Resources

About the consultant editor Lynn Wright
Lynn Wright is an editor and journalist with 20 years' experience in writing about computing, technology and digital photography.

Resources

Which?

www.which.co.uk/books

Other books available from Which?

Microsoft Excel 2010 Made Easy
ISBN: 978 1 84490 143 2
Price: £8.99

The ideal step-by-step guide to using Microsoft Excel 2010 and mastering its latest features. Packed with time-saving shortcuts, screenshots and tips to help avoid common mistakes.

- Learn to set up spreadsheets for tracking household budgets
- Create pivot tables
- Display data graphically in charts
- Insert and edit images in your spreadsheets
- Get started with sparklines

PC Problem Solving Made Easy
ISBN: 978 1 84490 109 8
Price: £10.99

A practical handbook for every Windows 7 PC user that provides step-by-step instructions and advice on both troubleshooting and fixing your computer problems.

- Error messages explained
- Dealing with viruses and other security threats
- Retrieving lost files
- Stopping junk mail
- Jargon buster for technical terms
- Free access to the Which? Computing helpdesk

Computing Made Easy for the Over 50s: Windows 7 Edition
ISBN: 978 1 84490 112 8
Price: £10.99
Previous Vista edition ISBN: 978 1 84490 068 8

Step-by-step tutorials for those new to computers or to Windows 7, whether you are using a PC for the first time or upgrading from XP or Vista. Includes jargon busters for technical terms.

- Send emails and surf the internet
- Stay safe online
- Start using Microsoft Word and Excel
- Manage photos, videos and music
- Upgrade to Windows 7 from Windows XP or Vista

Internet Made Easy for the Over 50s
ISBN: 978 1 84490 075 6
Price: £10.99

The essentials of connecting to and using the internet safely, finding the information you want and keeping in touch online – all in straightforward, easy-to-follow steps.

- Connecting your equipment
- Searching, buying, selling and banking online
- Keeping your online identity safe
- Free access to the Which? Computing Helpdesk

Using Your PC Made Easy: Office 2010 and More
ISBN: 978 1 84490 125 8
Price: £10.99

Features easy-to-follow, fully illustrated tutorials showing just how much you can do with your PC. Covers Microsoft Office Home and Student 2010.

- Create professional-looking documents and eye-catching presentations in Microsoft Word and PowerPoint
- Use spreadsheets to calculate and display data in Excel
- Time-saving keyboard shortcuts
- Free access to the Which? Computing helpdesk

Laptops and Mobile Devices Made Easy
ISBN: 978 1 84490 117 3
Price: £10.99

Step-by-step tutorials, jargon busters and plenty of helpful tips explain the different types of gadget available and how to use them. Includes how to download and use apps and ebooks, maximising the potential of your mobile device.

- PC laptops, netbooks, MacBooks, smartphones, ebook readers, tablets and iPads
- Choosing the right device for your needs
- Connecting to the internet wirelessly
- Synchronising data and sharing media across devices